Gluten-Free

MORE THAN 100 DELICIOUS RECIPES YOUR FAMILY WILL LOVE

MICHAEL COX

A FIRESIDE BOOK
PUBLISHED BY SIMON & SCHUSTER
NEW YORK LONDON TORONTO SYDNEY SINGAPORE

Created and produced by:
Carroll & Brown Limited
20 Lonsdale Road
Queen's Park
London NW6 6RD

Managing Art Editor Adelle Morris
Editors Salima Hirani, Caroline Uzielli
Photographer David Murray

FIRESIDE
Rockefeller Center
1230 Avenue of the Americas
New York, NY 10020

Printed and bound in Italy by LEGO.

10 9 8 7 6 5 4 3 2 1

Library of Congress Cataloging-in-
Publication Data
Cox, Michael
    Gluten-free : more than 100 delicious
    recipes your family will love / Michael
    Cox.
      p. cm.
    Includes index.
    1. Gluten-free diet—Recipes. I. Title.
RM237.86 .C69 2000
641.5'63—dc21   00-024511

ISBN 0-684-87251-X

Contents

Introduction

If your body cannot tolerate gluten (found in wheat and related grains), to the great frustration of your palate, I'm pleased you picked up this book, as my aim here is to shatter the myth that a gluten-free diet means you have to give up all the fun there is to be had in food—the appreciation of flavors and the pleasure taken in sharing a good meal with family or friends. Sadly, this myth is a reality for many who suffer from this intolerance, known medically as the celiac condition. Many of the gluten-free cookbooks on the market place much emphasis on the limitations of the diet, rather than providing any useful inspiration, so it is unsurprising that people often feel doomed to a lifetime of boring and rather lonesome meals. My personal experience of gluten-free cooking has been remarkably positive—I have found that the possibilities of the diet are endless, if you alter your attitude to food slightly and are willing to broaden your repertoire of ingredients. Far from being a handicap, a gluten-free diet can be very satisfying. Meals can be stylish, sophisticated and enjoyed by anyone, not just those who happen to have an intolerance to wheat.

REDISCOVERING COOKERY

My interest in food and cooking began in my first job, when I designed cookbooks with the cookery writer Katie Stewart for Paul Hamlyn, the publisher. When I was diagnosed with the celiac condition I was devastated. The knowledge that my body could not tolerate an ingredient that was part of my everyday diet was unbelievable. But the practical implications only began to sink in slowly as I realized that foods such as bread, pasta and cakes cannot be made with any real success using the substitutes that exist for wheat products. Familiar doors began to close. But I realized that if I didn't want to settle for a second-rate diet, I would have to rethink my attitude to food.

At that time in my life I was lucky enough to travel quite extensively. Discovering how cooking was approached in other parts of the world was a great learning curve for me which opened many new doors. I became aware of the great wealth of gluten-free ingredients that I had not known of before, or that I had neglected in the past in favor of more familiar wheat-based products. I also discovered new ways of cooking rice, cornmeal and other grains containing the complex carbohydrates necessary in a gluten-free diet. I began to rely more on legumes and nuts. Things that had always been part of my diet—meat, fish, eggs, milk, cheese, fruits and vegetables—were easily and tastily combined with the ingredients that were taking the place of wheat, rye, barley and oats.

As my interest in and knowledge of nutrition grew, I became intent on eating better in a broader sense and began substituting olive oil for butter, yogurt for cream, and made good use of vegetables and legumes for fiber. My new attitude to cooking was given an irresistible challenge when my partner and I set up a small guest house in southern Spain. I was in charge of the catering and was determined (as a reaction to the days of boring and lonely gluten-free meals) not to cook separate meals for myself, so all the food was prepared without wheat. My intention was to create meals that were not only healthy, but also light, interesting and full of flavor—not too difficult with the availability of high-quality produce in Spain. Nobody seemed to notice the lack of wheat. In fact, I was well rewarded as the guest-house became very successful over our ten years there and the food, apparently, is renowned!

In this book I have gathered a personal selection of my most successful recipes from the guest-house. On the whole, these have been inspired by traditional Mediterranean cooking, in which the obvious lack of gluten first caught my attention and fired my imagination. I was keen to make my work in the kitchen as easy as possible by simplifying recipes whenever feasible, so the recipes are all quite easy to follow. Because the property is in a rural location, access to

THE CELIAC CONDITION

Celiacs suffer from an intolerance to gluten, found in wheat, and to similar proteins found in related grains—rye, barley and oats. An adverse reaction to gluten results in the lining of the small intestine becoming damaged. This reduces the body's ability to absorb enough goodness from food to keep the body going. Besides uncomfortable abdominal symptoms, fatigue, breathlessness, anemia and general nutritional deficiencies may arise. The only known cure is a strictly gluten-free diet.

THE GLUTEN-FREE DIET

There are two guidelines to follow. The first is to identify and eliminate the foods that obviously contain gluten. Consult your doctor as to what to avoid and use the chart here for quick reference. The second factor is to identify and avoid the foods in which gluten is an inconspicuous ingredient. Some manufacturers use chemically modified wheat flour or starch in their products. Read the ingredients labels and avoid products that contain the following: starch, edible starch, food starch, cereal binder, cereal filler, cereal protein, unspecified sweeteners and stabilizers. The Celiac Sprue Association has information on gluten-free foods. Contact them at CSA/USA, Inc., P.O. Box 31700, Omaha, NE 68131–0700. Tel: (402) 558 0600. email: celiacs@csaceliacs.org website: www.csaceliacs.org

DON'T CONTAIN GLUTEN

Build your diet around the following items:

Fruits and vegetables—either fresh, frozen or dried. Canned fruits and vegetables may also be eaten as long as they have only added salt and water.

Potatoes, rice, corn, buckwheat, tapioca, arrowroot and their products—the flours made from many of these products, along with cornmeal are all excellent substitutes for wheat flour and pasta.

Meat, game, poultry and seafood—fresh or cured. Canned fish as long as it is canned either in oil or water.

Legumes and nuts.

Dairy produce and eggs—all unprocessed dairy produce, powdered milk.

Oils and fats—all oils, butter, margarine and lard.

Condiments—salt, unprocessed pepper, herbs and spices, vinegar.

Soups—home-made soups made with gluten-free ingredients.

Cakes, sweeteners and preserves—sugar, honey, golden syrup, home-made cakes baked with gluten-free ingredients and raising agents, jams, jelly, marmalade, molasses and corn syrup.

Raising agents—yeast, cream of tartar, tartaric acid, baking soda.

DO CONTAIN GLUTEN

Grains—wheat, barley, rye, oats and their products, such as pastas, cereals, noodles, bran, semolina, bulgur, couscous and breads.

MAY CONTAIN GLUTEN

These items may have gluten-containing ingredients:

Dairy produce—all cheese-based spreads, yogurt, processed milk products.

Condiments and flavourings—pepper compounds, mustard powder, soy sauce, all prepared sauces, pickles, chutneys, salad dressings and stock cubes.

Meat, game, poultry and seafood—all canned, precooked and packaged products, such as pâté, sausages and sausage rolls, and coated, frozen fish.

Cakes, confectionery, desserts and preserves—all precooked and packaged cakes, pastries and biscuits, all sweets and chocolates, mincemeat, peanut butter, lemon curd, all ready-made desserts.

Miscellaneous—baking powder.

NUTRITIONAL KNOW HOW

A sufficient intake of protein is vital to good health and especially important in the diets of children and pregnant or breastfeeding women. In an ordinary diet, protein will come from dairy produce, eggs, meat, fish, and bread and flour. The celiac has to watch his or her protein levels, as intake will be reduced due to gluten-intolerance—the vegetarian or vegan celiac must be even more vigilant. Make sure you consume extra dairy products, eggs, meat and fish. Legumes combined with nuts also yield protein. Wheat products also contain energy-producing carbohydrates that must be replaced in the diet of a celiac. Substitute these with gluten-free flour, rice, potatoes, sugars and fats.

specialized gluten-free products was impossible, so hardly any are required for the recipes included in this book (see the notes on ingredients, opposite). Each chapter contains a mixture of recipes that make excellent family fare, as well as those that are suited to entertaining. Chapter 1, for instance, provides a good range of soups and appetizers for all seasons, both rustic and sophisticated. In Chapter 2, you will find a collection of light meals, all of which are ideal for either lunch or a light evening meal. This chapter also contains useful advice on how to make the most of rice and polenta—both staple alternatives to wheat—and also contains a section on legumes. In Chapter 3, a range of healthy and satisfying entrées will tempt your palate. Chapter 4 contains a selection of dishes that can be served either as vegetarian main meals, or as vegetable side dishes, depending on the quantities you make, of course. This section will be useful to refer to time and time again when looking for the perfect accompaniment to a meal. I have also included in this chapter a small section on gluten-free savory sauces. Chapter 5 contains all my favorite desserts! There are gluten-free fruit tarts, meringues, iced desserts and so on. The flavors of the Mediterranean come through strongly here, in recipes that marry figs with honey and wine, or oranges with dates. I wish someone had given me a copy of Chapter 6—Cakes & Breads—when I was first diagnosed with the celiac condition—it wouldn't have seemed nearly as bad then! This is my wheat-free approach to baking that many of our guests enjoyed—I hope you do too! Throughout the book I have suggested ways in which recipes can be varied to produce different, yet equally delicious results.

Although the main inspiration for these recipes is both the wealth and the quality of the ingredients and traditional cooking of the Mediterranean, I must also acknowledge the invaluable guidance of some of the most renowned cooks of our time in the compilation of this book, most notably of Elizabeth David, Claudia Roden and Delia Smith.

Notes on Ingredients

The majority of the ingredients used in this book are readily available in grocery stores, supermarkets or failing that, health food stores. When purchasing baking powder, bouillon cubes and mustard, it is important to remember that they may not be gluten-free as manufacturers often add flours and wheat products to aid the preparation process. (French mustard is usually gluten-free, so I have used Dijon mustard in my recipes.) When buying these products, always read the labels to identity suspect ingredients (see page 7).

1

Soups & Appetizers

TZATZIKI

1 large cucumber, peeled and seeded

Salt to taste

1 cup Greek yogurt*

2 cloves garlic, peeled and crushed

Chopped fresh mint (optional)

Olive oil for drizzling

This delicious cucumber, yogurt and garlic dip is a popular Greek starter that can be served with crudités and chips or used as a relish for many main dishes such as kebabs, grilled fish or vegetables.

Grate the peeled cucumber and sprinkle with salt—this draws out excess moisture. Leave the cucumber to drain in a sieve for at least 1 hour. Transfer the cucumber to a bowl and mix in the yogurt, crushed garlic and chopped fresh mint (if using). Drizzle olive oil over the dip and chill before serving. (*Available at gourmet stores and Middle Eastern markets.)

HUMMUS

1¾ cups chickpeas (cooked or canned)

7 tablespoons Tahini

2–3 cloves garlic, crushed

Juice of 1 lemon

⅓ cup olive oil, plus extra for drizzling

Salt and pepper to taste

Gluten-free paprika and chopped fresh parsley to garnish

Tahini added to a base of chickpea purée gives this popular Middle Eastern dip its distinctively strong flavor (see right, in bowl).

1 If using dried chickpeas, soak them overnight, then boil them in plenty of water until tender.

2 Drain the cooked or canned chickpeas and set aside the liquid. Place the chickpeas in a bowl with the other ingredients. Mash with a fork into a thick purée or blend in a food processor. If the paste seems too thick, use some of the chickpea cooking water (or liquid from the can) to dilute it. The consistency should be like that of mashed potatoes. Season to taste.

3 Spoon the hummus into a bowl, drizzle a little olive oil over it and sprinkle with a pinch of paprika and some parsley. Place the bowl in the center of a large dish and surround with crudités, potato and tortilla chips to serve.

GUACAMOLE

2 ripe avocados

Juice of 1 lemon or 2 limes

1 small tomato, finely chopped

1 small green bell pepper, seeded and finely chopped

1 shallot, peeled and finely chopped

Handful of chopped fresh cilantro

Dash of Tabasco sauce (or pinch of chili powder)

Good as a dip, sauce, topping or side dish, this Mexican speciality is made of mashed avocados, lemon or lime juice and various seasonings (see right, on plate). I like it quite spicy but you can tailor it to suit your own taste. Serve guacamole with crudités, poppadums or tortilla chips. It is especially delicious with fresh shrimp—peel them, but leave the tails on so they are easier to hold and dip.

Mash the avocados roughly with a fork and add the lemon or lime juice. Mix in the rest of the ingredients to create a smooth but textured consistency. Season the guacamole to taste with the Tabasco sauce (or chili powder)—bear in mind that this dip should be fairly hot but not fiery. To store before serving, cover with plastic wrap placed directly on the surface and refrigerate to prevent the avocado flesh from discoloring.

Dips are great for informal first courses and as tasty additions to a light lunch or picnic. There are many gluten-free alternatives to the breads that usually accompany these dips. Crudités (chopped raw vegetables, such as carrot and celery sticks, radishes, cucumber and zucchini spears, bell pepper strips, mushrooms, cauliflower florets, etc.) are the perfect accompaniment as well as being very nourishing. Poppadums (which are made from gram or lentil flour and are therefore gluten-free) make a tasty alternative to potato and tortilla chips. To add a touch of class, shrimp—with the tails left on—are great for dipping.

There are no firm rules for following these recipes. What I have set out to do is give basic guidelines for some well-known appetizers. Herbs, oil, garlic, pepper, lemon juice or other ingredients can be replaced, added or taken away, according to individual taste. The recipes given here should each make enough for approximately 4 servings.

TAPENADE

This Provençal paste, made from black olives, capers and anchovies, can be served with a variety of crudités or used as an accompaniment to meat and fish dishes.

1 Drain the pitted black olives and blend in a food processor very briefly until they are roughly chopped. Alternatively, chop them by hand into very small pieces.

2 Add the capers, chopped anchovies (with oil from the tin to taste), garlic, olive oil, lemon juice and herbs. Process or mash into a fairly rough paste—this dip should not be too smooth. Season generously with freshly ground black pepper. (Salt may not be necessary as the anchovies are very salty.) Serve with tortilla chips or a variety of crudités.

¾ pound black olives, pitted

4 tablespoons capers

2 ounce can anchovy fillets, chopped

1 clove garlic, crushed

6 tablespoons extra virgin olive oil

Juice of 1 lemon

10–12 leaves basil, finely shredded, or dried oregano

Black pepper to taste

MELON & YOGURT SOUP

1 medium-sized melon (any variety)

4 ounces (small carton) plain yogurt

4 tablespoons lemon juice

1 teaspoon grated fresh ginger root

Chopped fresh mint to serve

Serves 4

This low-calorie soup has a refreshing clean taste. The fact that it is quick to make also recommends it, especially for last-minute meals.

1 Cut the melon in half, remove the seeds and scoop out the flesh. You should have approximately 1 quart (4 cups) of melon pulp.

2 Mix together the melon, yogurt, lemon juice and ginger root in a food processor or blender, process until smooth, and chill well until ready to serve. Sprinkle with chopped fresh mint before serving.

GAZPACHO

2¼ pounds ripe tomatoes, peeled (see Baked Cod with Tomatoes, page 32)

1 small cucumber, peeled and seeded

1 small green bell pepper

2 cloves garlic, peeled and crushed

Pinch of salt

6 tablespoons sherry (or wine) vinegar

½ cup light olive oil

Chopped cucumber, onion, bell pepper, tomatoes and hard-boiled eggs to serve

Serves 4–5 (makes 1 quart or 4 cups)

The best of all summertime soups! The traditional Andalusian recipe uses stale breadcrumbs, but this gluten-free version works equally well without them.

1 Chop the tomatoes, cucumber and bell pepper. Place in a food processor or blender along with the garlic, salt and vinegar and blend thoroughly.

2 Gradually add the olive oil and continue blending or stirring the mixture until it is smooth and creamy. If the consistency is too thick, dilute it with a little water.

3 Chill well before serving. When ready to serve, add chopped cucumber, onion, red or green bell pepper, hard-boiled eggs, tomato and a few Polenta Croutons (see page 47).

AJO BLANCO

1 cup whole blanched almonds

4 cloves garlic, peeled

2 cups water or milk

Pinch of salt

⅔ cup light olive oil

3 tablespoons sherry vinegar

Grapes, melon balls or diced apple to serve

Serves 4

A creamy white garlic soup (see right), this is usually made with stale bread. As with gazpacho, I do not add the bread, nevertheless the result is simply delicious.

1 Blend the almonds, garlic, water (or milk, which makes a richer soup) and salt in a food processor or blender.

2 Gradually stir in the oil, then the vinegar. Add more salt if necessary. This soup is traditionally served with sliced grapes, but melon balls or diced apples are equally good.

CARROT & ORANGE SOUP

1 medium-sized onion, peeled

1 pound carrots

3 tablespoons olive oil

3½ cups chicken or vegetable stock

1 teaspoon sugar

Salt and white pepper to taste

Juice of 4 oranges

Chopped fresh mint or snipped chives to garnish

Serves 6

The oranges give this soup a very clean and crisp taste. Carrot and orange soup is perfectly refreshing for a hot summer's day and delicious served sprinkled with chopped fresh mint or chives.

1 Chop the onion and carrots and place in a saucepan. Add the oil and sweat the vegetables for roughly 10 minutes. (To sweat the food, cover the pan with the saucepan lid and cook over low heat to allow the food to cook in its own juices without browning.)

2 Pour in the stock. Add the sugar, salt and pepper. Bring to a boil and simmer covered for 1 hour or until the carrots are very soft.

3 Remove from the heat and purée the mixture in a food processor or pass through a sieve, then allow to cool.

4 Add the orange juice, then chill thoroughly in the refrigerator. Serve garnished with mint or chives.

EGGPLANT SOUP

2¼ pounds eggplant (3 or 4, depending on size)

1 large onion, peeled

1 red bell pepper, seeded

2 medium-sized ripe tomatoes

6 tablespoons olive oil

Salt and black pepper to taste

2 cloves garlic, peeled and chopped

1 teaspoon dried thyme

1 teaspoon dried oregano

1 bay leaf

1 quart (4 cups) vegetable or chicken stock

Juice of 1 lemon

Saffron Mayonnaise (see page 19) or gluten-free sour cream to serve

Serves 4

The roasted vegetables and garlic give this soup its unique flavor which can be enjoyed either hot or cold.

1 Preheat the oven to 400°F, 200°C, gas mark 6. Chop all the vegetables roughly and brush them with some of the olive oil. Add salt and freshly ground pepper and place them in a fairly deep roasting pan. Put in the top of the oven, where it is hottest, for 30 minutes or until the edges of the vegetables are slightly charred, which will give the soup a strong flavor.

2 In a large saucepan, gently sauté the chopped garlic with the herbs in the remaining oil for about 5 minutes until browned.

3 Add the roasted vegetables to the garlic and herbs and stir well until thoroughly mixed.

4 Add the stock and slowly bring to a boil. Simmer covered for about 30–40 minutes until the vegetables are thoroughly cooked and soft.

5 Remove from the heat and place in a food processor or pass through a sieve to purée. Add the lemon juice and adjust the seasoning to taste.

6 If serving the soup cold, chill in the refrigerator, then present with a dollop of Saffron Mayonnaise (see page 19) on each portion. A swirl of sour cream goes well with a hot serving.

SPINACH & LEMON SOUP

The flavors of the lemon and garlic complement the spinach in this lively appetizer. A swirl of sour cream adds an extra tang to the appeal.

1   If using fresh spinach, wash the leaves and remove any large stalks. Melt the butter in a large saucepan and add the onion and garlic. Cover and cook over low heat until translucent, not browned. Add the spinach and continue to cook for a further 5 minutes.

2   Pour the chicken stock over the vegetables, season with salt and pepper, then cook for a further 10 minutes until the vegetables are soft.

3   Remove from the heat and place in a food processor or pass through a sieve to purée. Adjust the seasoning and add the lemon juice. Reheat and serve with a spiral of sour cream and a sprinkling of grated nutmeg.

1 pound fresh (½ pound frozen) spinach

½ stick (4 tablespoons) butter

1 onion, peeled and chopped

2 cloves garlic, peeled and crushed

3⅓ cups chicken stock

Salt and pepper to taste

Juice of 1 lemon

Gluten-free sour cream and grated nutmeg to serve

Serves 4

RICH TOMATO SOUP

This combination of cooked tomatoes and crème fraîche or pesto creates a rich, filling soup (see right) which can be both a winter warmer or a refreshing summer starter, as it can be served either hot or cold.

1   Chop the vegetables roughly. If the tomatoes are not fully ripe, enhance the flavor by adding a few sun-dried tomatoes that have been soaked in hot water for 1–2 hours.

2   Place all the vegetables in a large saucepan and add the garlic, olive oil and bay leaves, followed by the peppercorns and salt. Cover and stew gently in the pan for 1 hour or until all the vegetables are very soft and pulpy. Stir the mixture occasionally during cooking to ensure it does not stick to the bottom of the pan, but do not add water or stock as the tomatoes contain enough liquid to make the soup.

3   Once all the vegetables are soft and thoroughly cooked, take off the heat, remove and discard the bay leaves and place the cooked vegetables in a food processor or pass through a sieve to purée.

4   Adjust the salt to taste, if necessary. If serving hot, add a swirl of crème fraîche to each serving; if serving cold, a tablespoon of Pesto Sauce (see page 90) can be added for extra flavor and color. A mixture of both crème fraîche and pesto swirled on the top also makes an attractive garnish.

2¼ pounds very ripe tomatoes

1 large carrot, washed

1 medium-sized onion, peeled

3 sticks celery, with leaves left on

1 clove garlic, peeled and chopped

1 tablespoon olive oil

2 bay leaves

A few peppercorns

Salt to taste

Serves 4

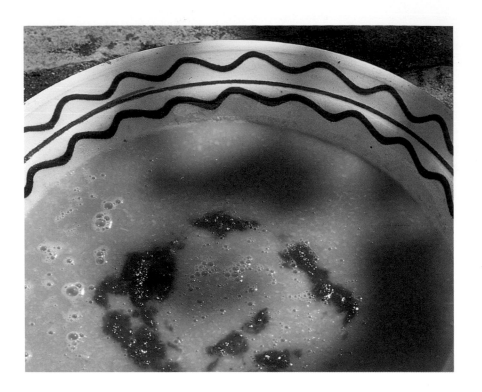

SWEETCORN SOUP WITH CHILI SAUCE

FOR THE SOUP

4 ears fresh corn (14 ounces frozen)

½ stick (4 tablespoons) butter or 3 tablespoons olive oil

1 onion, medium-sized, peeled and chopped

1 quart (4 cups) vegetable/chicken stock

Salt and pepper to taste

FOR THE CHILI SAUCE

6 red chilies, seeded and chopped

1 clove garlic, peeled and crushed

Handful of chopped fresh parsley

Pinch of salt

½ cup extra virgin olive oil

Serves 4

This sweet soup works brilliantly with a hot flash of chili sauce (see above), which enlivens the taste with a Latin American flavor.

1 To cook the ears of corn, place them in a large saucepan of water and boil for 15 minutes. (For frozen corn, cook according to packet instructions.) Once cooked, strip the corn kernels from the ear with a sharp knife.

2 Place the butter or olive oil in a saucepan and gently sweat the chopped onion for a few minutes until translucent. Add the corn, stir well and cook for a few more minutes.

3 Add the stock and gradually bring to a boil. Simmer covered for 20–30 minutes or until the corn is tender.

4 Once cooked, season with salt and pepper, then blend in a food processor. For a smoother soup pass through a sieve or a food mill. Adjust the seasoning to taste. Allow to cool and chill, if serving cold.

5 To make the chili sauce, pound the chilies, garlic, parsley and salt roughly in a mortar with a pestle, working in the oil a little at a time.

6 If serving hot, return the soup to the saucepan and slowly reheat. Serve the soup either hot or cold with a swirl of chili sauce.

AVGOLEMONO SOUP

This popular Greek soup has a light, lemony flavor, yet the addition of the rice and eggs makes it a satisfying starter.

1 Boil the rice in the stock for 12–15 minutes until tender. Once cooked, remove from the heat and leave the rice in the liquid. Beat the egg yolks with the lemon juice in a bowl. Add a little of the hot stock and beat again.

2 Pour the egg mixture into the hot rice broth, return to a low heat and whisk vigorously until thickened, ensuring it does not boil (or the eggs will curdle). Once heated through, serve immediately, garnished with parsley.

⅓ cup long-grain rice

1 quart (4 cups) chicken stock

4 egg yolks

Juice of 1 lemon

Chopped fresh parsley to garnish

Serves 4

FISH SOUP WITH ARTICHOKES

The success of this soup depends entirely on the quality of the fish stock. For best results I always recommend a home-made stock prepared from fresh bones and trimmings.

1 Prepare the fish stock (see below) in advance. To make the soup, place the monkfish pieces and the quartered artichoke hearts in boiling fish stock. Add the saffron, reduce the heat and simmer for 20 minutes until the artichokes are tender and the fish is cooked.

2 Serve immediately with a dollop of Saffron Mayonnaise (see below) and sprinkled with chopped fresh parsley.

1 quart (4 cups) fish stock

½ pound monkfish, boned and cut into pieces

½ pound artichoke hearts, quartered (fresh or canned)

Pinch of gluten-free saffron

Saffron Mayonnaise (see below) and chopped fresh parsley to serve

Serves 4–5

SAFFRON MAYONNAISE
Follow the recipe for Garlic Mayonnaise (see page 90), adding a pinch of dried and powdered gluten-free saffron (see below). Saffron mayonnaise tastes wonderful in many soups and with shellfish.

DRIED AND POWDERED SAFFRON
To maximize the flavor and color of saffron, dry strands by wrapping them in foil and placing them in a moderate oven for 10 minutes. Once cool, powder them with your fingers. Use to flavor sauces and rice.

FISH STOCK
Break up 1 pound of fish bones and trimmings, wash thoroughly and place in a large saucepan with 1 quart (4 cups) of cold water and ½ cup of dry white wine. Add a teaspoon of salt and bring to a boil. Peel and chop 2 cloves of garlic, 1 small onion, 2 sticks of celery and 1 carrot. Once the liquid boils, add the vegetables with a handful of chopped fresh parsley, 1 bay leaf and 6 white peppercorns. Simmer covered for 20 minutes, until all the vegetables are soft. Strain and use as a base for soups, sauces and casseroles. Keep in a container for up to 2 days in the refrigerator or freeze for up to 3 months.

SQUID SALAD

The flavor of the squid is delicately set off by the chili, lemon and garlic dressing in this appetizer that is good for any special occasion.

1   Clean the squid thoroughly in cold water and slice the bodies into ½ inch-thick rings.

2   Pour the lemon juice into a pan of boiling water and plunge the squid into the water for 1 minute only, then drain immediately. Do not overcook the squid or it will become tough.

3   Heat the oil in a separate saucepan until very hot. Drop in the sliced garlic and chilies and sauté them for 1 minute or so until the garlic turns golden brown and the chilies are crispy. Remove from the heat and allow to cool.

4   Season the cooked squid with salt and plenty of freshly ground black pepper. Pour the cooled oil, garlic and chili mixture over the squid and mix well to ensure that all of the squid is covered in the dressing. Divide the squid into 4 portions and serve with lemon wedges and a watercress and arugula salad.

1 pound baby squid

Juice of 1 lemon

1⅓ cups olive oil

6 cloves garlic, peeled and sliced

3 green chilies, seeded and sliced

Salt and black pepper to taste

1 lemon cut into wedges to serve

Serves 4

SEAFOOD SALAD

Fresh mussels, squid and shrimp dressed in garlic and lemon make a substantial appetizer or a delicious light lunch. I love to use a mixture of crisp lettuce leaves to complement the fish in this salad.

1   Thoroughly scrub the mussels under cold running water with a small stiff brush and discard any that have damaged shells. Steam them open by placing them in a covered pan on a rack or steamer over simmering water for 5 minutes. Once cooked, remove the mussels from their shells. Discard any that have not opened.

2   Clean the squid in cold water and slice into ½ inch-thick rings. Plunge them into a pan of boiling water for no more than 1 minute and drain immediately. Do not overcook them or they will become tough.

3   If the shrimp are uncooked, plunge them into the boiling water for 1 minute until they turn pink. Drain immediately, cool, then shell them.

4   Combine the cooked mussels, squid, shrimp and chopped celery in a large mixing bowl and dress with the crushed garlic, olive oil, lemon juice and salt and pepper.

5   Divide the chopped lettuce into 4 portions and arrange on plates. Place the fish on top and garnish with plenty of chopped fresh parsley to serve.

2 pounds mussels

½ pound baby squid

½ pound shrimp

2 sticks celery, chopped

2 cloves garlic, crushed

3 tablespoons olive oil

Juice of 1 lemon

Salt and pepper to taste

1 lettuce of any variety, chopped

Chopped fresh parsley to garnish

Serves 4

SHRIMP & MELON SALAD

This splendid combination of fresh shrimp, juicy, sweet melon and lively flavorings (see above) makes a salad that is a perfect appetizer for an outdoor meal on a hot summer evening.

1 To cook the shrimp, plunge them into boiling water for 1–2 minutes, then allow them to cool. Peel the shrimp, leaving their tails on. Cut the melon in half and scoop out the flesh using a melon baller. Alternatively, cut the flesh into cubes. Place the melon pieces in a bowl with the cooked shrimp and chopped celery.

2 Make the dressing—mix together the mayonnaise, lemon juice, curry powder, ginger and cayenne pepper. Stir well and pour over the shrimp and melon. Mix thoroughly to ensure all the ingredients are evenly coated with the dressing. Allow to stand for at least 15–30 minutes, then divide into 4 portions and serve with snipped fresh chives if desired.

1 pound fresh shrimp

1 cantaloupe

2 sticks celery, chopped

½ cup mayonnaise

Juice of 1 lemon

1 tablespoon gluten-free curry powder

1 teaspoon grated ginger root

Pinch of gluten-free cayenne pepper

Snipped fresh chives to garnish (optional)

Serves 4

MUSSELS WITH SALSA

The salsa topping adds a splash of color and additional flavor to these mussels, which are eaten directly from their shells (see left). They make an eye-catching appetizer for special occasions.

1 Scrub the mussels thoroughly under cold running water with a small, stiff brush and discard any that have damaged shells. Steam them open by placing them in a covered pan on a rack or steamer over simmering water for 5 minutes. Remove the mussels from their shells and reserve 16 of the cleanest half-shells. Discard any mussels that have not opened.

2 For the salsa, finely chop the tomato, onion or shallots and the bell pepper and place in a bowl. Pour the olive oil and lemon or lime juice over the chopped vegetables, then season with salt and pepper.

3 Mix the mussels with the salsa and allow to marinate in the refrigerator for at least 30 minutes.

4 When ready to serve, arrange the half-shells on a plate and, using a small spoon, place one mussel and a little salsa in each half-shell. Avoid placing too much liquid in the shells, as this may spill during serving and ruin the presentation. Sprinkle each filled shell with finely chopped fresh cilantro or parsley—the green looks very attractive against the red salsa. The mussels should be eaten by hand, directly from the shell.

16 large mussels

1 small, firm tomato

1 small onion or 2 shallots, peeled

1 small green bell pepper

1 tablespoon olive oil

Juice of 1 lemon or 2 limes

Salt and pepper to taste

Finely chopped fresh cilantro or parsley to garnish

Serves 4

SWEETCORN FRITTERS

Similar to small pancakes or blinis, sweetcorn fritters (see inset, left) make a lovely first course. Serve them hot with sun-dried Tomato Pesto mixed with crème fraîche. They are also delicious cold and are ideal for taking on picnics or serving with dips and drinks.

1 Beat the eggs in a bowl, then add the crème fraîche and continue beating until the two are thoroughly blended. Add the cornmeal (or polenta) and mix well, making sure there are no lumps—if there are any lumps present, beat them out with a spoon. Once the mixture becomes a smooth batter, tip in the drained sweetcorn kernels and continue to mix.

2 Meanwhile, heat a little oil in a roomy, non-stick skillet and drop a few tablespoons of the cornmeal, egg and crème fraîche mixture into the pan. Be careful not to overcrowd the pan—instead, cook the fritters in a few batches. Cook them for 2–3 minutes, then flip them over carefully and cook the other sides for a further 2–3 minutes. Drain on paper towel to absorb any excess oil, then keep them warm while cooking the rest. Allow roughly 2–3 fritters per portion. Serve with a generous dollop of crème fraîche mixed with Tomato Pesto (see page 90).

2 eggs

3 tablespoons crème fraîche

3 tablespoons cornmeal or fine polenta

1⅓ cups cooked sweetcorn (or an 11-ounce can), drained

Oil for frying

Crème fraîche and Tomato Pesto (see page 90) to serve

Serves 4 (makes 12 fritters)

SPINACH ROULADE

FOR THE ROULADE

I pound cooked spinach, chopped
(2¼ pounds fresh or frozen spinach)

5 eggs, separated

4 tablespoons light cream

Freshly grated nutmeg to taste

Salt and pepper to taste

FOR THE FILLING

¾ cup cream cheese

¾ cup crème fraîche

¼ pound smoked salmon trimmings

Black pepper to taste

Serves 8

Spinach roulade makes an impressive appetizer (see below) that is simple to prepare and keeps well for a day or two. Cook and drain the fresh spinach the day before it is needed if possible, to minimize the moisture content. Frozen spinach can also be used for this dish.

1   Preheat the oven to 400°F, 200°C, gas mark 6. Grease a 15½ x 10½-inch jelly roll pan and line it with wax paper, making sure the lining overshoots the edges of the pan a little.

2   Place the cooked and chopped spinach in a bowl. Make sure it is as dry as you feel is possible.

3   Mix the egg yolks, cream, nutmeg, salt and pepper into the spinach. Beat the egg whites until stiff, but not too dry and fold into the spinach mixture.

4   Spread the mixture evenly on to the lined jelly roll pan and bake in the oven for 15 minutes. To check that the roulade is cooked, press it gently in the middle with your finger—if the sponge springs back into shape, it is cooked. If your finger leaves an impression, cook for a further 5 minutes.

5 Remove the pan from the oven and leave to stand for 5 minutes. Turn out on to a sheet of aluminium foil that is larger than the roulade and carefully peel off the wax paper lining. It does not matter if a little of the spinach sticks to the paper.

6 To make the filling, mix the cream cheese and crème fraîche with the salmon trimmings and season with freshly ground black pepper.

7 While the spinach base is still warm, spread the cream cheese mixture on to it, gently roll up the roulade and wrap it in foil. Do not worry if the roll cracks a little, or if some of the filling squeezes out.

8 Allow the roulade to cool completely, then slice and serve. Sour cream or mayonnaise thinned into a thin sauce with some water—or a mixture of both—makes an excellent accompaniment.

MOLDED GAZPACHO

This dish is based on the traditional soup but without the bread and with gelatin added to help it take shape. Molded gazpacho looks impressive set either in a large ring mold or in small oval dariole molds or ramekins for single portions.

1 Dissolve the gelatin in 3 tablespoons of very hot water in a small saucepan. (Always add the gelatin powder to the liquid, never the other way around.) Stir vigorously and allow to stand for 1–2 minutes, then, if not completely dissolved, place over very low heat for a few seconds and stir. Do not allow the liquid to boil. Once it is transparent and runny, allow to cool and add lemon juice to dilute further.

2 Place the tomatoes, bell pepper, shallots and garlic (if using) along with the vinegar and olive oil in a food processor. Process until everything is blended into a smooth and creamy mixture. Alternatively, pass the ingredients through a sieve and mix. Add the dissolved gelatin and stir again for a moment. Season with salt and pepper.

3 Transfer the gazpacho to a jug and wait until it begins to set. Stir from time to time to stop the mixture from separating. You should have approximately 1 quart (4 cups) of liquid.

4 As the gazpacho begins to set, pour it into a 3 cup ring mold or into six ⅔ cup ramekins or oval dariole molds. Chill for several hours.

5 When ready to serve, loosen the molded gazpacho with a hot, sharp knife and turn out on to a large serving dish, or on to individual dishes if using smaller molds. Serve with the chopped bell peppers and Saffron Mayonnaise (see page 19), which has been thinned with a little water.

3½ teaspoons (about 1½ envelopes) unflavored gelatin

A squeeze of lemon juice

4 medium-sized very ripe tomatoes, peeled (see Baked Cod with Tomatoes, page 32) and seeded

1 small green bell pepper, seeded and chopped

2 shallots, peeled and chopped

1 clove garlic, peeled and crushed (optional)

3 tablespoons white wine vinegar

3 tablespoons olive oil

Salt and pepper to taste

Saffron Mayonnaise (see page 19) and a few chopped mixed bell peppers to serve

EGG & CUCUMBER TERRINE

This light terrine can be made in individual molds or set in a loaf tin, then sliced. It makes an attractive first course, especially when decorated with a little cress or slices of cucumber (see right).

3½ teaspoons (about 1½ envelopes) untlavored gelatin

1 cup plain yogurt

3 tablespoons mayonnaise

Juice of 1 lemon

Salt and pepper to taste

Dash of gluten-free Tabasco sauce

5 eggs, hard-boiled

1 large cucumber, peeled and seeded

Sliced cucumber to serve

Serves 6

1   Dissolve the gelatin in 4 tablespoons of very hot water in a small saucepan. (Always add the gelatin powder to the liquid, never the other way around.) Stir vigorously and allow to stand for 1–2 minutes, then, if not completely dissolved, place over very low heat for a few seconds and stir. Do not allow the liquid to boil. Once it is transparent and runny, allow it to cool and add a small squeeze of the lemon juice to dilute further.

2   Mix together the yogurt, mayonnaise and the remaining lemon juice and season with salt and pepper to taste. Add a dash of Tabasco sauce (taking care not to make the mixture too hot), then stir in the dissolved gelatin.

3   Peel and chop the hard-boiled eggs and dice the cucumber finely. Place these in a bowl and carefully fold in the liquid mixture.

4   Spoon the terrine mixture into 6 six oiled ⅔ cup ramekins or oval dariole molds, or into an 3 or 4 cup loaf tin. Chill thoroughly for several hours.

5   Once the terrine has set, slide a sharp, heated knife around the edges of the terrine to loosen it from the mold. Turn out on to individual plates if using the smaller molds, or on to a serving dish if using the loaf tin. Serve with the cucumber slices or a green salad.

CHICKEN LIVER PÂTÉ

Smooth and creamy chicken liver pâté always goes down well as an appetizer or lunch dish. Spread it thickly on freshly baked Herb and Olive Bread (see page 122).

½ stick (4 tablespoons) butter

1 small onion, peeled and chopped

1 clove garlic, peeled and chopped

½ pound chicken livers

1 tablespoon chopped fresh thyme (or mixed herbs)

1 tablespoon brandy

Freshly grated nutmeg to taste

Salt and pepper to taste

Oil or chopped fresh parsley to garnish

Serves 4–6

1   Melt the butter in a skillet. Add the onion and garlic and cook gently until the onion is translucent. Chop up the livers, removing any veins and sinews. Add the chopped livers to the frying onions and garlic and cook together for 10 minutes until the livers are cooked through. Add the thyme and the brandy and cook for a further 1–2 minutes.

2   Place in a food processor (or a bowl, if using a hand-held blender). Grate a little nutmeg over the livers and season with salt and pepper, then process until smooth and creamy.

3   Spoon into a small terrine (or another suitable dish) and allow to cool. Cover the top of the pâté with a little oil to prevent it looking dry once it has cooled. Alternatively, cover the surface with chopped fresh parsley.

AVOCADO MOUSSE & SHRIMP SAUCE

FOR THE MOUSSE

3½ teaspoons (about 1½ envelopes) unflavored gelatin

2 large, very ripe avocados, peeled

½ cup plain yogurt

½ cup mayonnaise

Juice of 2 limes

Salt if necessary

Tabasco sauce or cayenne pepper to taste

6 jumbo shrimp, cooked and peeled

Oil for greasing

FOR THE SHRIMP SAUCE

½ pound shrimp, cooked and peeled

3 tablespoons mayonnaise

Juice of 1 lime

Salt and pepper to taste

Chopped fresh parsley to garnish

Serves 6

This light mousse, served with a creamy, flavorful sauce makes an elegant first course. I like to set the mousse in six small molds rather than one large one, as this makes for a neater presentation.

1 Dissolve the gelatin in ¼ cup of very hot water in a small pan. (Always add the gelatin powder to the liquid, never the other way around.) Stir vigorously and allow to stand for 1–2 minutes, then, if not completely dissolved, place over very low heat for a few seconds and stir. Do not allow the liquid to boil. Once it is transparent and runny, allow to cool and add the juice of one lime to dilute further.

2 Coarsely chop the avocados and place them in a food processor with the yogurt, mayonnaise, the remaining lime juice, salt and Tabasco (or cayenne pepper) and blend into a fine cream. Or, place everything in a bowl and blend with a hand-held blender. Add the dissolved gelatin and mix well.

3 Lightly grease six ⅔ cup individual molds (oval dariole molds or custard cups or ramekins are ideal). Place one jumbo shrimp on the base of each mold. Pour in the avocado mixture and chill in the refrigerator for at least 2 hours, until set.

4 Meanwhile, make the shrimp sauce. You do not need shrimps of the best quality for this, as they will be puréed—properly thawed frozen shrimps will be more than adequate. Place these in a food processor with the mayonnaise and lime juice, adding 1–2 tablespoons of water to dilute. Process until the sauce has the consistency of heavy cream. If you do not have a food processor, chop the shrimp into very small pieces and mix them with the other ingredients using a hand whisk. Season with salt and pepper to taste.

5 Once the mousse has set, run a sharp, heated knife around the molds and carefully turn out the mousses on to individual plates. To serve, pour some shrimp sauce around each mousse and garnish with a sprinkling of chopped fresh parsley.

GUACAMOLE MOUSSE
Prepare the avocado mousse as instructed in step 2, above. Substitute the shrimp sauce with a vegetable and vinaigrette dressing. Place half a peeled, seeded, and diced cucumber, 1 seeded and diced red bell pepper, 1 peeled and finely chopped onion and 1 chopped tomato into a bowl and mix together well. Add 2 tablespoons of Vinaigrette (see page 91) and a sprinkling of chili powder. Mix together until all the vegetables are thoroughly coated in the dressing. Place a large spoonful on each plate with the avocado mousse and garnish with a handful of chopped fresh cilantro.

Fish Mousse

This mousse is very simple to make. Although smoked salmon (trimmings are more economical), smoked mackerel or smoked trout produce sublime results, any type of fish can be used—try a different variety each time to experiment. Unsmoked white fish may taste a little insipid, so a few anchovy fillets can be incorporated for added flavor.

3½ teaspoons (about 1½ envelopes) unflavored gelatin

1 pound fish, smoked or cooked

Juice of 2 lemons

1 cup plain yogurt

3 tablespoons mayonnaise

Salt and black pepper to taste

1 tablespoon chopped fresh herbs such as parsley or tarragon (optional)

3 egg whites

Cucumber, peeled, seeded, and thinly sliced, and watercress to serve

Serves 6

1 Dissolve the gelatin in ¼ cup of very hot water in a small saucepan. (Always add the gelatin powder to the liquid, never the other way around.) Stir vigorously and allow to stand for 1–2 minutes, then, if not completely dissolved, place over very low heat for a few seconds and stir. Do not allow the liquid to boil. Once it is transparent and runny, allow to cool and add the juice of one lemon to dilute further.

2 Place the fish, the remaining lemon juice, yogurt, mayonnaise, salt (which may not be necessary if using smoked fish or anchovies) and black pepper in a food processor and combine until smooth. (Alternatively, blend the mixture in a bowl using a hand-held blender.) Add the cooled gelatin and mix well. If using a food processor, transfer the mixture into a bowl. Stir in the chopped fresh herbs.

3 Beat the egg whites in a separate bowl until stiff but not dry, then fold the beaten egg whites into the fish mixture gently, taking care not to beat the air out of them.

4 Divide the mousse into 6 portions and spoon each of these portions into an ⅔ cup oval dariole mold or ramekin, or spoon the entire mixture into an 3 or 4 cup loaf tin. Chill in the refrigerator for several hours to set.

5 When ready to serve, slide a sharp, heated knife between the mousses and the molds (or loaf tin) to loosen them. Turn out on to individual plates or a large serving dish and decorate with thinly sliced cucumber and bunches of watercress.

HAM MOUSSE

Prepare the gelatin as instructed in step 1, above. Mix 1 cup of yogurt with 3 tablespoons of mayonnaise and 3 tablespoons of gluten-free Dijon mustard in a bowl. Add the dissolved gelatin. Mix well, then mix in 1 pound of cooked minced ham and season with salt and pepper to taste. (Ham tends to be fairly salty, so it may not be necessary to add salt.) For a light mousse, fold in 2 stiffly beaten egg whites. For a more solid, terrine-like texture, omit the egg whites.

Thinly slice 3–4 gherkins lengthwise and arrange the slices on the base of an 3 or 4 cup loaf tin. Spoon the ham mixture over the top of the gherkins and chill for at least 2 hours before serving. Slide a sharp, heated knife between the terrine and the mold and carefully turn out on to a plate. Decorate with a few gherkins and serve.

2

Lunches & Suppers

FISH

POULTRY

MEAT

CHEESE & EGGS

RICE

POLENTA

LEGUMES

BAKED COD WITH TOMATOES

The crisp, sunny taste of fresh tomatoes is the essence of this dish (see left). As with any tomato recipe the quality of the fruit is paramount. If good tomatoes cannot be obtained, a simple tomato sauce may be used, but the recipe will not retain the freshness that brings it to life.

1 Preheat the oven to 350°F, 180°C, gas mark 4. Grease a 8 x 12 inch gratin dish with oil. To peel the tomatoes, make a small incision in the skin of each one, then plunge them into boiling water for 15–20 seconds. Lift them out using a slotted spoon and plunge them straight into cold water. Allow them to sit in the cold water for about 1 minute, then remove. The skins should now come away from the flesh easily (if not, return them to the boiling water for a further 20 seconds). Roughly chop the peeled tomatoes.

2 Heat 2 tablespoons of olive oil in a saucepan over medium heat and soften the onion and garlic in the oil. Once translucent, not brown, add the tomatoes, then the bay leaf and dried oregano. Season with salt and pepper to taste. Slowly bring the mixture to a boil and allow to simmer for no more than 5 minutes, so the tomatoes are not reduced to a pulp, but remain fairly chunky.

3 Cut the cod fillet or fillets into suitable sizes for individual portions, each weighing roughly 7 ounces. Place these in the oiled gratin dish and season with salt and pepper.

4 Pour the hot tomato stew over the pieces of cod and bake in the preheated oven for 15–20 minutes, until the fish is tender and the sauce is bubbling. Garnish with chopped hard-boiled eggs and chopped fresh parsley and serve with boiled new potatoes and a green salad.

Oil for greasing

1 pound ripe tomatoes

2 tablespoons olive oil

1 large onion, peeled and chopped

2 cloves garlic, peeled and chopped

1 bay leaf

1 teaspoon dried oregano

Salt and black pepper to taste

1¾ pound cod fillet (or fillets)

2 eggs, hard-boiled, chopped, to garnish

Handful of chopped fresh parsley to garnish

Serves 4

BAKED HALIBUT OR TURBOT STEAKS

Other filleted fish such as haddock or pollack can be used in the same way as the cod fillets in the recipe above. However, fish steaks such as halibut or turbot, although a little extravagant, can also be used just as successfully. These should be cooked a little longer, for about 30 minutes.

BAKED FISH PACKAGES

Fillets of cod, haddock and pollack, or steaks of halibut and turbot can be baked in packages to retain their flavor and moisture. Make a paste in a mortar using a pestle by grinding together 6 tablespoons of olive oil, 2 chopped shallots and 4 tablespoons of chopped mixed herbs such as parsley, dill and basil. Add a little salt and freshly ground black pepper to taste. Cut 4 sheets of aluminum foil or parchment to a size that is slightly larger than that of the fish and place a fillet or steak on each sheet. Cover with the herb paste and wrap it in the foil carefully, tucking in the ends. Place the packages on an oiled baking sheet and bake in a preheated oven for 20–30 minutes (depending on the fish) at 400°F, 200°C, gas mark 4. Serve in their packages with lemon wedges.

Fish Pie

This dish is best when made with a variety of fish and shellfish. Smoked haddock gives the sauce additional flavor and shrimp add a lively splash of color. Include some hard-boiled eggs and top the dish with mashed potato to give it texture and body. Fish pie is a family favorite which is both nutritious and filling.

1 Preheat the oven to 400°F, 200°C, gas mark 6. Grease a 6-cup ovenproof pie dish with melted butter.

2 Wash and peel the potatoes, then cut them into pieces. Place in a saucepan and cover with water. Add salt and bring to a boil. Reduce the heat and simmer for 15–20 minutes until the potatoes are soft, then drain well. Mash the potatoes in the saucepan with the butter and milk until smooth, adding salt and pepper to taste. Meanwhile, place the eggs in a small saucepan of water and bring to a boil. Reduce the heat and simmer for 6 minutes until nearly hard-boiled, then allow to cool.

3 Place the cod and haddock in a saucepan with the milk, bay leaf, onion and peppercorns. Bring the mixture to a boil, then remove from the heat. Cover the pan and leave to stand in a warm place for 10 minutes to allow the fish to cook through and the milk to be infused with the flavor of the fish, creating a deliciously aromatic liquid for the sauce. Remove the fish with a slotted spoon and set aside to cool. Strain the cooking liquid and reserve.

4 Make a white sauce—dissolve the cornstarch in 2 tablespoons of cold milk and stir into the hot infused milk. Slowly bring the liquid to a boil, stirring continuously, then simmer for 1 minute before adding the lemon juice. Remove the sauce from the heat and set aside. It should have a fairly thick consistency.

5 Flake the cooked fish, carefully removing any skin and bones. Place the flakes in the white sauce and add the cooked shrimp. Season with salt and pepper and add a little grated nutmeg and dill, if desired. Gently fold the fish into the sauce until thoroughly mixed.

6 Shell the boiled eggs and cut in half. Lay the halved eggs on the base of the greased pie dish, then spoon the fish mixture over the top. Cover the fish with a layer of mashed potato and decorate the top surface with wavy fork marks. Bake in the preheated oven for 30 minutes until the potato topping is brown and the sauce is bubbling. Serve immediately with a green salad or a vegetable side dish.

Butter for greasing

1¼ pounds potatoes

Pinch of salt

2 tablespoons butter and ½ cup milk for mashing potatoes

Salt and white pepper to taste

2 large eggs

½ pound cod fillet

½ pound smoked haddock

1 quart (4 cups) milk

1 bay leaf

1 small onion, peeled and chopped

A few black peppercorns

⅓ cup cornstarch

3 tablespoons cold milk

Juice of 1 lemon

¼ pound shrimp, peeled and cooked

Freshly grated nutmeg to taste (optional)

Chopped fresh dill to taste (optional)

Serves 4

CRUNCHY CRUMBLE TOPPING
Replace the potato topping with a crunchy crumble topping: blend 1 cup of cornmeal, 6 tablespoons of butter, 1 tablespoon of freshly grated Parmesan and some chopped fresh parsley. Sprinkle over the fish mixture and bake as above.

CHICKEN WITH BASIL & ALMONDS

4 boneless, skinless chicken breast halves (about 1½ pounds)

3 tablespoons olive oil

1 cup ground almonds

2 cloves garlic, peeled and crushed

¾ cup finely shredded fresh basil, plus extra to garnish

Juice of 1 lemon

1¼ cups sour cream

Salt and pepper to taste

Serves 4

Succulent chicken breasts are accompanied in this dish by a vibrant green basil sauce, thickened with ground almonds and sour cream, with garlic and lemon juice for added flavor. This nourishing supper can be made very quickly and easily.

1   Combine the olive oil with 2–3 tablespoons of water in a large skillet, add the chicken breasts and gently poach without browning them over medium-low heat for 10 minutes on each side.

2   Meanwhile, make the sauce—mix the ground almonds, garlic, basil, lemon juice and sour cream into a smooth sauce, in a food processor, or with a wooden spoon in a bowl. Season with salt and pepper.

3   Once the chicken is almost cooked, pour in the sauce, mixing it with the juices in the pan. Cook for a further 10 minutes until the sauce has heated through. Garnish with basil and serve with brown rice or boiled potatoes.

CHICKEN, AVOCADO & YOGURT MAYONNAISE

FOR THE CHICKEN

1 medium-sized cold, cooked chicken (4–5 pounds, roasted or poached)

2 ripe avocados

Chopped fresh cilantro to garnish

FOR THE YOGURT MAYONNAISE

¾ cup plain yogurt

⅓ cup mayonnaise

Juice of 1 lemon

1 tablespoon gluten-free curry powder

1 teaspoon ground coriander

Salt and black pepper to taste

Serves 4

This lunch dish is ideal for scorching hot days, which is often the case in the Spanish summer. The spicy, slightly tangy mayonnaise is both light and refreshing and works well with cold chicken. Serve with Spicy Moroccan Rice (see page 68).

1   Remove the skin from the chicken and discard. Separate the flesh from the bones and cut it into bite-sized pieces. Place the pieces in a large bowl.

2   To make the sauce, mix the yogurt with the mayonnaise, lemon juice, curry powder and ground coriander and beat until smooth. Leave to stand for at least half an hour to allow the sauce to be infused by the spices.

3   Pour the sauce into the bowl with the chicken pieces and mix well to cover all the pieces of chicken thoroughly in sauce. Add salt and freshly ground black pepper to taste.

4   Cut the avocados into quarters lengthways, then into eighths, removing the skin as you go. Wet the flesh with lemon juice to stop it discoloring.

5   To serve, place the sauce in a large shallow serving dish and sit the chicken in the sauce. Arrange the avocado wedges around the chicken. Sprinkle the entire dish liberally with chopped cilantro.

CHICKEN FRIED WITH ROSEMARY & GARLIC

In this simple recipe the chicken pieces are cooked in garlic and fresh rosemary (see above)—a light and tasty combination that is good hot or cold. This dish is ideal for picnics.

1   Season the pieces of chicken with salt and pepper to taste. Heat the oil in a heavy-based skillet over medium heat and fry the chicken pieces in the oil for approximately 15 minutes until fairly brown and crispy. Make sure you turn them from time to time so that they are evenly cooked and browned all over.

2   Add the garlic and rosemary to the pan and continue to sauté for a further 10–15 minutes. Remove from the pan and serve immediately with sautéed potatoes and vegetables, or allow to cool and serve cold as part of a picnic or summer lunch with Pesto Rice (see page 59) and a tossed green salad.

1 medium-sized chicken (4–5 pounds), cut into 8 pieces (thighs or legs)

Salt and pepper to taste

3 tablespoons olive oil

6 cloves garlic, peeled and sliced

Handful of chopped fresh rosemary leaves

Serves 4

ENDIVE & HAM GRATIN

The bitter taste of Belgian endive adds a pungency to this ham and cheese gratin.

4 endives, cut in half horizontally

Pat of butter, about ½ tablespoon

8 slices smoked ham

1⅓ cups Cheese Sauce (see page 91)

¼ cup freshly grated Parmesan cheese

Serves 4

1 Preheat the oven to 425°C, 220°C, gas mark 7. Trim the endives and place them in a large saucepan that has a lid with the butter and 2–3 tablespoons of water. Cover and cook over low heat for 20 minutes, turning once, until tender. Add more water as necessary. Once cooked, allow to cool slightly.

2 Lay the slices of ham on a chopping board and place a piece of cooled endive on each slice. Wrap the ham around each endive.

3 Arrange the wrapped endive and ham pieces in a deep ovenproof dish and pour over the cheese sauce. Sprinkle with the Parmesan cheese.

4 Bake in the top half of the preheated oven for 20–30 minutes, until the cheese topping is golden brown and the endives are tender. Serve immediately, with boiled new potatoes or baked potatoes, if desired.

BEEF PIE WITH OLIVES & RAISINS

This is a gluten-free version of the popular English favorite, Shepherd's Pie, a delicious hot dish of flavored ground meat topped with mashed potatoes. Here, green olives and raisins are added to the ground beef which gives this dish an exotic twist.

3 tablespoons olive oil

1 pound ground beef

1 small onion, peeled and chopped

1 medium-sized carrot, chopped

1½ tablespoons cornstarch

1⅓ cups beef stock

1 tablespoon tomato purée

1 teaspoon dried, mixed herbs

Salt and black pepper to taste

25 pitted green olives

¼ cup seedless raisins

Mashed Potatoes (see page 72)

Serves 4–6

1 Preheat the oven to 400°F, 200°C, gas mark 6. Heat the oil in a skillet and add the ground beef. Cook over high heat for 5 minutes, stirring occasionally, until the meat is evenly browned.

2 Stir the chopped onion and carrot into the pan with the meat and cook for a further 10 minutes. Sprinkle the cornstarch into the pan and stir well to combine with the meat and vegetables.

3 Pour in the beef stock, add the tomato purée and mixed herbs and season with salt and black pepper. Stir the mixture again, then bring to a boil. Reduce the heat and simmer covered for 30 minutes, stirring occasionally until the meat is cooked through and the sauce has thickened. Finally stir in the olives and raisins.

4 Spoon the cooked meat mixture into a 8 x 12-inch ovenproof dish and cover with the mashed potatoes. Decorate the top surface with fork marks. Bake at the top of the preheated oven for 25–30 minutes until the potato topping is brown. Serve piping hot with a green vegetable.

BEEF SALAD WITH MUSTARD DRESSING

Cold cooked beef is mixed with gherkins and shallots and tossed in a mustard and red wine vinegar dressing for a dramatic blend of flavors. This salad is ideal for using up cooked leftover meat, but if you do not have any, use grilled steak or ham as an alternative.

1 Cut the beef into strips of about 2 x ½-inches. Place them in a large mixing bowl with the chopped gherkins and shallots.

2 To make the dressing, place the oil, vinegar, mustard, sugar and garlic in a separate bowl. Blend with a whisk or hand-held blender until the mustard is combined with the oil and vinegar and the dressing is smooth. If it is too thick, add a tablespoon of cold water.

3 Pour the dressing over the beef and stir. Add salt and pepper to taste (salt may not be necessary as the mustard can be quite salty). Leave to stand for at least 30 minutes before serving to allow the meat to absorb the flavor of the mustard. Garnish with chives and serve with a crispy green salad.

1¼ pounds cold cooked beef

3 tablespoons gherkins, chopped

2 shallots, peeled and chopped

⅔ cup vegetable or olive oil

7 teaspoons red wine vinegar

3 tablespoons gluten-free Dijon mustard

½ teaspoon sugar

1 clove garlic, peeled and crushed

Salt and pepper to taste

Snipped fresh chives to garnish

Serves 4

PORK WITH TUNA & YOGURT SAUCE

This cold dish of tender pork slices topped with a creamy tuna and anchovy sauce is my version of the classic Italian dish "Vitello tonnato" which is based on veal. I prefer to use pork as I feel it has more flavor and I use yogurt in place of cream in the sauce for a lighter result.

1 Preheat the oven to 400°F, 200°C, gas mark 6. Wrap the pork tenderloin in foil and place in a roasting pan surrounded with a little water. Roast in the oven for 60–85 minutes until cooked through but not dry. To check the joint is cooked, pierce it with a sharp knife through to the middle and if the juices run clear, the meat is cooked. Remove the pork from the oven and allow to cool, keeping it wrapped in the foil to ensure it does not dry out.

2 To prepare the tuna sauce, place the tuna fish (and its oil) in a mixing bowl with the anchovies, yogurt, mayonnaise and lemon juice. Season with black pepper to taste, but not with salt as the fish is salty enough. Blend the mixture with a hand-held blender or in a mortar with a pestle until it has the consistency of heavy cream.

3 When ready to serve carve the cold meat into thin slices and arrange on a serving plate. Pour the sauce over the meat and scatter the capers on the top. Serve with cold Lentil and Grilled Pepper Salad (see page 48).

FOR THE PORK

2¼ pounds boneless pork tenderloin

FOR THE TUNA SAUCE

4 ounces canned tuna in oil (⅔ of a 6-ounce can)

2 anchovy fillets

½ cup plain yogurt

1 tablespoon mayonnaise

Juice of ½ lemon

Black pepper to taste

3 tablespoons capers to garnish

Serves 6

SOUFFLÉ

This basic soufflé recipe is an excellent example of how successfully cornmeal can be used as a substitute for wheat flour. No matter how simple, a soufflé is always impressive, but there are many interesting possibilities when it comes to selecting flavorings. Make sure your sauce is thick initially, and then lightened by the stiffly beaten egg whites. This produces a well risen soufflé that makes an ideal first course or lunch dish.

1 Preheat the oven to 400°F, 200°C, gas mark 6. Grease a 6-cup soufflé dish with a little melted butter. Melt the remaining butter in a large pan and stir in the cornmeal. Cook for 1–2 minutes. Gradually pour in the milk, stirring continuously until it is blended smoothly with the cornmeal. Simmer for 3 minutes, stirring constantly—this prevents lumps from forming in the sauce. Set aside to allow the mixture to cool slightly.

2 Mix in the egg yolks, the flavoring (see below) and seasonings. Make sure you select seasonings that work well with your chosen flavoring. For instance, nutmeg works well with the flavours of cheese and smoked fish, and herbs such as parsley go well with puréed vegetables. Salt and pepper work well with most flavors.

3 Beat the egg whites (which should be at room temperature) until stiff and dry. Fold a little of the beaten egg whites into the sauce, then carefully fold in the rest. Take care not to knock the air out of the egg whites as you mix them in, as it is the air that causes the soufflé to rise and gives it the light, airy texture it is known for.

4 Sprinkle either the freshly grated Parmesan cheese or polenta into the base of the greased dish—this keeps the soufflé mixture stuck to the sides of the dish as it cooks, which helps it to rise. Pour in the soufflé mixture. Bake in the preheated oven for 35–40 minutes—make sure the soufflé does not overcook and become dry. Wobble the dish carefully to check whether or not the centre is set. Serve immediately.

---

2 tablespoons butter, plus extra for greasing

2 tablespoons cornmeal

1 cup milk

4 large eggs, separated, at room temperature

3–4 ounces flavoring such as grated cheddar cheese, fish or puréed vegetables

Seasonings, such as salt and pepper to taste and a pinch of freshly grated nutmeg or a herb, where appropriate

1 tablespoon freshly grated Parmesan cheese or 1 tablespoon polenta

Serves 4

FLAVORINGS

If using cheese or fish, use strongly flavored varieties. Mature cheddar is best for cheese soufflés—it should be grated and added to the basic sauce. Smoked salmon or smoked haddock are good fish choices. Poach the fish, then mash it with a fork and add to the basic sauce.

To add a lively hint of color, spinach or watercress can be used. The leaves should first be wilted, then broken down in a food processor or mashed with a fork before being added to the basic sauce. If using vegetables with a delicate flavor, add some cheese, such as freshly grated Parmesan. Broccoli is also a delicious vegetable for using in soufflés. To prepare, steam the broccoli florets for 2–3 minutes until just tender, then rinse in cold water and chop finely. Add to the basic sauce with some chopped, fried shallots and crumbled blue cheese.

CHEESE & ONION TART

The classic combination of cheese and onion always works a treat. In my gluten-free version of this tart, cornmeal is used to make a pastry shell, which is baked blind before being filled and baked again.

FOR THE PIE PASTRY SHELL

1 cup cornmeal

½ stick (4 tablespoons) butter, chilled and cut into small pieces

1 large egg, beaten

Pinch of salt (if the butter is unsalted)

FOR THE CHEESE & ONION FILLING

4 large eggs

½ cup heavy cream or plain yogurt

4 ounces mature cheddar, grated or blue cheese, crumbled

Pepper to taste

Freshly grated nutmeg to taste

1 medium-sized onion, peeled and thinly sliced

Pat of butter

Serves 4–6

1 Preheat the oven to 350°F, 180°C, gas mark 4. Blend the cornmeal and butter, either in a food processor or by crumbling the butter into the cornmeal with your fingers until the mixture resembles breadcrumbs. Once the cornmeal and butter are well blended, mix in the salt (if using).

2 Add the beaten egg to the mixture to make a dough. If the pastry is too dry and crumbly, add a drop or two of water to help it bind together. Shape the dough into a ball with your hands.

3 Place the pastry ball between two sheets of plastic wrap and flatten it with the base of your palm. Roll it out into a fairly even sheet of pastry large enough to line a 10-inch tart pan. Remove the top sheet of plastic wrap and, using the lower sheet, lift up the pastry and turn it over on to the tart pan. Remove the plastic wrap and press the pastry into the pan, working it across the base and up the sides. Cut off excess pastry and use it to patch up broken or thin areas. Handle the pastry as little as possible. If using 4 or 5 inch tartlet pans for individual servings, line as many as you can, then shape the leftover pastry into a new ball. Re-roll this between sheets of plastic wrap and use to line the remaining pans.

4 Place the pan (or pans) on a baking sheet in the preheated oven. Bake for approximately 15 minutes.

5 Meanwhile, make the filling—blend the eggs, cream (or yogurt) and grated or crumbled cheese together in a food processor, or mix them thoroughly in a bowl using a hand whisk. Add the pepper and grated nutmeg. (Salt will not be necessary as the cheese is salty enough.)

6 Remove the pastry shell from the oven and set aside to cool slightly. Meanwhile, melt the butter in a skillet and sauté the sliced onion until softened, but not browned. Place in the cooked pastry shell (or shells).

7 Pour the egg mixture on to the onions and place on a baking sheet. Bake in the preheated oven for 30 minutes if using a large tin, or 20 minutes if using small tartlet pans. In either case, ensure the filling is cooked in the middle before removing from the oven. Allow to cool a little before serving, or serve cold, with a mixed salad.

BACON AND CHEESE TART

Replace the onions with 3 slices of smoked bacon, cut into cubes, and fry in a little oil over high heat for 2–3 minutes until cooked, but not crispy. Scatter these over the pastry shell, then pour in the filling and bake as above.

TORTILLA

This substantial omelette—known in Spain as the "Tortilla"—is a vital part of the traditional Spanish tapas (see above). Warm, freshly cooked tortilla is delicious on its own or with grilled meat and fish. Slices of cold tortilla, served with a green salad, make excellent picnic fare.

1   Gently sauté the potatoes and the onion (if using) in 3 tablespoons of the oil in a large non-stick skillet for 20 minutes, until the potatoes start to break up. Avoid browning or burning them.

2   Whisk the eggs in a bowl and season with salt and pepper. Transfer the cooked potatoes—while still hot—to the bowl containing the eggs and mix well, ensuring the potatoes are thoroughly coated with the egg mixture. (The trick with making a proper tortilla is to place the hot potatoes into the eggs, not vice versa.)

3   Heat the remaining oil in a smaller (8 inch) non-stick skillet and spread the mixture evenly over the base by gently shaking the pan. (The eggs and potatoes are, traditionally, placed back into the original skillet, but the method given here results in a thicker, more moist omelette.)

4   Gently cook the tortilla over low heat for 10 minutes. Once the first side is browned, place a plate over the tortilla and turn the skillet upside-down, then slide the tortilla back into the skillet with the cooked-side facing up. Or cook the second side under a hot broiler, but ensure the omelette does not burn. Allow to cool a little before serving.

1 pound potatoes, peeled and sliced

1 onion, peeled and chopped (optional)

6 tablespoons olive oil

4 extra large eggs

Salt and pepper to taste

Serves 4

RISOTTO

This basic risotto can accompany grilled meat or fish dishes or may be served on its own as a main course, sprinkled with plenty of grated Parmesan. Vegetables, cooked with the rice, add color and texture. Risotto is only as good as its stock—make sure it has a strong flavor.

1   Heat the butter and/or oil in a saucepan and cook the onion and garlic until the onion is translucent, not brown. Add the rice and stir until the grains are thoroughly coated and become slightly translucent. Add the wine and heat until the rice has absorbed the liquid.

2   Pour in the hot stock, stir and bring slowly to a boil. Reduce the heat and simmer uncovered, stirring occasionally for 18–20 minutes, until the liquid is absorbed and the rice is *al dente*, or firm to bite. Risotto should be creamy in texture, so add a little more stock if necessary.

3   Mix in half the grated Parmesan cheese and season with freshly ground black pepper. (Salt is probably unnecessary as the cheese is quite salty.) Sprinkle the remaining cheese over the risotto and serve immediately.

4 tablespoons butter or 3 tablespoons olive oil (or an equal mixture of both)

1 small onion, peeled and chopped

1 clove garlic, peeled and chopped

1½ cups risotto rice such as Arborio or Pastariso

½ cup dry white wine

3⅔ cups hot chicken or vegetable stock

½ cup freshly grated Parmesan cheese

Black pepper to taste

Serves 4 (or 6 as a side dish)

CHOOSING THE RIGHT RICE

Rice is versatile—it absorbs flavors and can be served as a meal in itself or as an accompaniment to many dishes. It is a good staple in a gluten-free diet. Of the many types of rice, two are most widely used in cooking—long-grain and short-grain. Long-grain rice is good either boiled or steamed, plain or flavored. For the recipes here, use Basmati rice or any variety of American long-grain rice. Short-grain rice absorbs moisture but does not become soggy, hence is used for risottos. It is coated in heated oil or butter before the cooking liquid is added. The Italian Arborio rice is best for risottos and the Spanish Valencian variety is my choice for paellas. Any short-grain rice may be used for the recipes here. Brown rice, either long- or short-grain, is unpolished rice, so is rich in fiber. It is slow to cook and does not absorb flavors as much as polished varieties. I do not recommend precooked or instant rices.

COOKING LONG-GRAIN AND MEDIUM-GRAIN RICE

For 4 servings, use 1¼ cups of rice, 1⅔ cups of water and salt to taste. Wash and drain the rice and place in a saucepan with the water and salt. Bring to a boil, then simmer covered for exactly 10 minutes from the start of boiling. Remove from the heat and fluff with a fork—the liquid should be absorbed. Cover and leave to stand for 2–3 minutes before serving.

FLAVORING LONG-GRAIN RICE

To enhance plain boiled rice: use stock instead of water for a rich flavor; add a bay leaf and a knob of butter to the cooking water for fragrant rice; for a dramatic color and a wonderfully musty flavor, add a pinch of saffron; add a couple of segment-sized pieces of orange peel to the cooking water for tangy, perfumed rice—sprinkle with slivers of toasted almonds to serve.

RISOTTO CROQUETTES

3 eggs

8 cups cooked cold Risotto (see page 43)

3 tablespoons cornmeal (optional)

Handful of chopped fresh parsley

Oil for frying

Makes approximately 12 croquettes

These fried risotto patties (see inset, right) are delicious served with fresh Tomato Sauce (see page 55). Serve them hot as an appetizer, or cold as a snack or as part of a picnic. Allow 2–3 croquettes per person.

1 Beat the eggs and mix them into the cold risotto. Add the cornmeal (which helps to bind the grains of rice together) and the chopped fresh parsley. Mix thoroughly using a fork.

2 Divide the mixture into 12 portions and shape each into an 3-inch long patty, roughly ¾-inch thick. Heat the oil in a heavy-based skillet and add the patties. Fry them over medium heat for approximately 5 minutes until crisp and brown underneath. Turn the patties carefully and fry the other sides for a further 5 minutes. Drain on a sheet of paper towel and serve either immediately with Tomato Sauce (see page 55) or ketchup, or allow to cool and serve as a snack.

ASPARAGUS RISOTTO

2 tablespoons olive oil

1 small onion, peeled and chopped

1 clove garlic, peeled and chopped

¼ pound thin asparagus spears, stems trimmed

1½ cups risotto rice such as Arborio or Pastariso (see page 43)

½ cup dry white wine

Generous pinch of saffron strands, dried and powdered (see page 19)

3⅔ cups chicken or vegetable stock

Salt and pepper to taste

A hint of saffron and a few asparagus spears transforms a basic risotto into this bright and colorful dish (see right).

1 Heat the oil in a medium-sized saucepan. Add the onion and garlic and cook gently until soft. Chop the asparagus stalks. Reserve the tips and add the stalks to the pan. Fry with the onion and garlic for 1–2 minutes, then add the rice. Stir until the grains are fully coated in the oil and are slightly translucent. Add the wine and reduce over high heat until the rice has absorbed the liquid.

2 Dissolve the dried and powdered saffron (see page 19) in the hot stock and add this to the rice. Stir the mixture and bring to a boil, then reduce the heat and simmer uncovered for 10 minutes, stirring occasionally. Add the asparagus tips and cook for a further 8–10 minutes. The rice is cooked when the liquid is absorbed and the rice is creamy and *al dente*, or firm to bite. Add salt and pepper to taste and remove from the heat. Serve immediately.

MUSHROOM RISOTTO

To make a mushroom risotto, substitute the asparagus with 1 ounce of dried mushrooms soaked in ½ cup of hot water. Add the drained mushrooms to the onions, garlic and rice in the saucepan and pour over the hot stock and mushroom water (instead of the wine). Cook as for Asparagus Risotto, above, omitting the saffron. Once the rice is cooked, stir in a pinch of freshly ground nutmeg, salt and pepper and serve with a topping made from ¼ cup of freshly grated Parmesan cheese.

POLENTA

1 quart (4 cups) water

1 teaspoon salt

1⅓ cups polenta (or cornmeal)

Black pepper to taste

Freshly grated nutmeg to taste (optional)

Makes 8 slices

Used widely in Northern Italian cooking, polenta is a gluten-free Godsend. It has endless possibilities and makes a good substitute for rice or potatoes. Bear in mind that its strength is its texture, so serve it with a strong-tasting ingredient or spicy sauce. The recipe that follows is for standard polenta, but you can buy instant polenta which is just as good and easier to cook—just follow the packet instructions.

1 Place the water in a large saucepan, add the salt and bring to a boil. Then pour the polenta gradually into the boiling water, stirring constantly.

2 Reduce the heat and simmer for 30 minutes, stirring constantly to avoid burning. When it has a thick consistency and pulls away from the sides of the pan easily, remove the polenta from the heat, season with black pepper and nutmeg, if desired. Either use immediately or spoon into a 1 quart (4 cups) loaf tin, allow to cool, then turn out and slice.

INSTANT, READY-TO-USE POLENTA

Instant polenta and ready-to-eat polenta (which comes vacuum packed) are both easy alternatives to making your own polenta and are just as good. Both are available from gourmet stores. Follow the packet instructions.

POLENTA CROUTONS

Cut polenta slices into small dice and deep-fry them in vegetable oil until crispy. Drain on paper towel and use in thick soups and salads.

POLENTA AU GRATIN

Place prepared slices of polenta in a deep flameproof dish, cover with fresh Tomato Sauce (see page 55), sprinkle liberally with cheese and broil until the cheese bubbles (see right). Alternatively, top the slices with sautéed vegetables such as mushrooms and eggplant or with leftover ratatouille, sprinkle with freshly grated Parmesan cheese and broil. Try placing strips of grilled peppers and anchovy fillets on grilled slices of polenta and drizzle with olive oil.

POLENTA GNOCCHI

Gnocchi is an Italian dish that is usually based on potato, but polenta offers a delicious alternative. This version is very simple to prepare.

Oil for greasing

1 quart (4 cups) milk

1 large onion, peeled and studded with 1–2 cloves

1 bay leaf

Freshly grated nutmeg to taste

Pinch of salt

1 cup polenta or coarse cornmeal

3 egg yolks

1 cup freshly grated Parmesan cheese

Freshly ground black pepper to taste

Butter for greasing

Serves 4

1 Lightly grease a baking sheet with a little oil. Pour the milk into a large saucepan, add the onion and bay leaf, a little grated nutmeg and the salt. Bring to a boil, then reduce the heat to a low setting and simmer gently for at least 10 minutes. Remove the onion and bay leaf from the pan with a slotted spoon and discard.

2 Hold the bag or cup containing the polenta high above the pan and pour into the hot milk in a slow, steady stream, stirring constantly. Continue stirring and cook the mixture over low heat for 10 minutes or until it has a thick consistency and pulls away from the sides of the pan. Add some more milk if the polenta becomes too thick.

3 Remove from the heat and beat in the egg yolks, one at a time. Beat in half the grated Parmesan cheese and season with salt, lots of freshly ground black pepper and a little more grated nutmeg if desired.

4 Turn the polenta out on to the baking sheet and spread into an even layer, roughly ½-inch thick. Brush with melted butter, then leave to cool and set for at least 20 minutes. Meanwhile, preheat the oven to 450°F, 230°C, gas mark 8. Grease an ovenproof dish with melted butter.

5 When set, cut the polenta into 2-inch squares and place them, overlapping, in the ovenproof dish. Sprinkle the remaining Parmesan cheese over the gnocchi and bake in the top of the oven for roughly 15 minutes, until nicely browned. Serve with a salad tossed in a herb and garlic dressing.

LENTIL & GRILLED PEPPER SALAD

1¼ cups green lentils, Puy lentils if possible

3 bell peppers: 1 red, 1 green and 1 yellow, seeded

1 large onion, peeled

1 tablespoon oil

Salt and pepper to taste

Balsamic Vinaigrette (see below)

Handful of chopped fresh parsley to garnish

Serves 4–5

This attractive and substantial salad (see above) is delicious either cold or warm. Mixed chargrilled peppers add color and a strong flavor, which is intensified by the onions and Balsamic Vinaigrette.

1 Cook the lentils in plenty of boiling water for 20 minutes, until tender, then drain. Meanwhile, dice the bell peppers and onion, toss them in warmed oil and broil until the edges become a little charred—do not cook through.

2 Mix the cooked peppers and onion with the cooked warm lentils, season with salt and pepper and dress with Balsamic Vinaigrette (see below). Sprinkle with chopped fresh parsley and serve immediately.

TO MAKE BALSAMIC VINAIGRETTE
Place 4 parts of extra virgin olive oil, 1 part of balsamic vinegar, 1 clove of garlic, cut in half or, for stronger flavor, crushed, 1 teaspoon of mustard and salt and pepper in a jar with a lid and shake well. Adjust the seasoning to taste.

LENTIL & BACON STEW

Robust and spicy, this stew can be cooked in advance and successfully reheated, making it an ideal winter supper dish. Any variety of lentils can be used and they do not need to be soaked beforehand.

1 Chop the bacon into ½-inch pieces. Heat the oil in a Dutch oven or other heavy-based pot that has a lid and gently fry the bacon with the onion for 2–3 minutes. Add the crushed garlic, carrot, chili and ground coriander and continue to cook for a further 2–3 minutes.

2 Meanwhile, rinse and drain the lentils. Place them into the pot with the vegetables and flavorings and stir well to coat the lentils thoroughly with the mixture. Add the canned tomatoes with all the liquid from the can, then add the water and a pinch of salt.

3 Slowly bring the mixture to a boil, then reduce the heat and simmer covered for 40 minutes, until the lentils are soft. If the lentils become a little too dry, add a touch more water during cooking. Once cooked, remove from the heat and allow the stew to stand undisturbed for a few minutes before serving.

4 When ready to serve, heat a little oil in a skillet and cook the chopped garlic until golden brown, not burnt. Scatter the garlic over the stew and sprinkle with a little chopped fresh cilantro. Serve with plain white rice and a tossed green salad.

½ pound slab bacon, preferably smoked (use ham steak if less fat is desired)

3 tablespoons olive oil, plus extra for sautéing the garlic

1 small onion, peeled and chopped

2 cloves garlic, peeled and crushed

1 carrot, diced

1 green chili, seeded and chopped

1 teaspoon ground coriander

1¼ cups lentils

14½-ounce can of peeled tomatoes

2 cups water

Pinch of salt

3 cloves garlic, peeled and chopped

Chopped fresh cilantro to garnish

Serves 4–5

CHICKPEA SALAD WITH TUNA & ONIONS

Highly nutritious and tasty, this salad provides a good quantity of protein. It can be thrown together at the last minute if packaged precooked chickpeas and canned tuna are used.

1 Soak dried chickpeas overnight in plenty of cold water. Once soaked, place in a saucepan, cover with water and fast-boil for 10 minutes. Reduce the heat and simmer for 30 minutes, until tender. Drain and leave to cool. Alternatively, if using a can of chickpeas, simply drain before use.

2 Place the cold, cooked chickpeas in a bowl and flake the fish over them. Then pour the vinaigrette over the contents of the bowl, season with salt and pepper and mix well.

3 To serve, slice the onion very thinly and spread over the chickpea and tuna mixture. Garnish with the chopped fresh parsley.

1¾ cups cooked chickpeas (or 15-ounce can of chickpeas)

6 ounces fresh tuna, grilled or 6-ounce can of tuna

Balsamic Vinaigrette (see opposite)

Salt and pepper to taste

1 large red onion, peeled

Large bunch chopped fresh parsley

Serves 4–5

3 Entrées

FISH

POULTRY

BEEF

LAMB

PORK

SEAFOOD PAELLA

FOR THE STOCK

1 quart (4 cups) water

2 pounds mussels (in their shells)

½ pound raw shrimp

1 carrot, 1 leek and 2 sticks celery, chopped

2 bay leaves

Handful of fresh parsley stalks

10 peppercorns

FOR THE RICE

6 tablespoons olive oil

1 onion, peeled and cut into rings

2 cloves garlic, peeled and chopped

1 small green bell pepper, seeded and chopped

1 tomato, skinned and chopped

2 cups short-grain rice such as Valencia

Pinch of saffron strands, dried and powdered (see page 19)

1 quart (4 cups) dry white wine

Salt and pepper to taste

½ pound baby squid, cleaned

Lemon wedges to serve

Chopped fresh parsley to serve

Garlic Mayonnaise to serve (see page 90)

Serves 6

The mix of fresh seafood, rice and vegetables has made paella hugely popular far beyond the borders of Spain. Its characteristic yellow color is due to the powdered saffron. Meats such as chicken, pork, ham and chorizo (or spicy sausage) can also be added to make this into an even more robust and flavorful dish.

1   Bring the water to a boil in a large saucepan. Scrub the mussels under cold running water with a small, stiff brush, discarding any that are open or have damaged shells. Place in the boiling water until they begin to open, then lift them out and place in a colander to drain. Make sure the colander is sitting on a dish so you can collect the liquid that drains from the cooked mussels. This can be used when making the fish stock. Set the mussels aside and allow them to cool.

2   Plunge the shrimp into the boiling mussel water, then remove them almost immediately so they do not overcook and toughen. Allow to cool. Peel the shrimp, reserving the heads and shells, then set aside with the mussels. To make the stock, place the heads and shells back into the water and add the chopped carrot, leek, celery, bay leaves, fresh parsley stalks and peppercorns. Do not add salt, as the mussels themselves will provide a sufficient quantity. Simmer for 30 minutes then strain, reserving the liquid.

3   Meanwhile, heat the olive oil in a shallow, flameproof earthenware dish or paella pan (approximately 12 inches in diameter) and gently sauté the onion rings, garlic, pepper and tomato for approximately 5 minutes.

4   Add the rice and stir, making sure all the grains are well coated in oil. When the grains become slightly translucent, sprinkle on the dried and powdered saffron (see page 19) and add the dry white wine.

5   Pour the reserved fish stock on to the rice and stir. Check the seasoning, adding salt if necessary. Boil the mixture for 5 minutes, then reduce the heat and simmer uncovered for a further 15 minutes. From time to time, use a large spoon to maneuver the rice from the edges of the pan into the center, then stir.

6   About 5 minutes before the rice is cooked, when most of the liquid has been absorbed, place the uncooked squid into the simmering rice and stir. Arrange the cooked mussels and shrimp on the paella to heat. Add more water or wine if the dish becomes too dry.

7   Remove from the heat and allow the paella to rest for 5 minutes. The rice should be *al dente*, or firm to bite, but still moist. Do not worry if it sticks to the base of the pan a little.

8   Serve directly from the cooking dish, garnished with lemon wedges, chopped fresh parsley and Garlic Mayonnaise (see page 90).

FISH PILAF

1–1¼ pounds smoked or salted fish

3 eggs

4 tablespoons olive oil

1 small onion, peeled and chopped

2 cloves garlic, peeled and chopped

1 teaspoon ground cumin

1 teaspoon ground coriander

1 bay leaf

2–3 pieces lemon rind (pared with a potato peeler)

2 cups Basmati rice

Salt and black pepper to taste

Cayenne pepper to taste (optional)

2⅔ cups water

Juice of 1 lemon

Chopped scallions or snipped fresh chives to serve

Chopped fresh cilantro to garnish

Serves 4

Similar to the Anglo-Indian dish, kedgeree, this pilaf can be made using any fish that has a strong flavor, such as haddock or cod. Alternatively, try salted fish, which is often cod, and is known as "bacalao" in Spain and "baccalà" in Italy. You can use brown rice for a bulkier dish, but if you do, increase the cooking time to 30 minutes.

1   If you are using salted fish, soak it for 12–24 hours, changing the water every 4–5 hours. This process softens the flesh and reduces the level of salt in the fish with each change of water. Once you have drained the last batch of soaking water, pour some boiling water on to the fish, then cover and allow it to soak for roughly 15 minutes to allow the flesh to soften.

2   Place the eggs in a small pan of boiling water, return to a boil, then simmer gently for approximately 10 minutes. Remove the cooked eggs from the heat and drain, then plunge them into cold water. Allow to stand for a few minutes, then remove the shells and set aside the hard-boiled eggs.

3   Heat the olive oil over medium heat in a large skillet that has a lid. Fry the onion and garlic for 5 minutes, then add the cumin, coriander, bay leaf and lemon rind. Stir well to ensure that all the ingredients are thoroughly mixed.

4   Wash the fish and remove the skin. Cut the fish into 1–1¼-inch-long chunks and add these to the pan. Mix all the ingredients together well and continue to cook for 1 more minute.

5   Wash the rice thoroughly and drain, then tip it into the pan with the fish, stirring continuously to ensure that all the grains are properly coated in oil and spices. Season the mixture generously with salt and pepper and add as much cayenne pepper as you wish, according to how spicy you would like to make the pilaf.

6   Pour in the water and bring slowly to a boil. Mix everything thoroughly, then reduce the heat and simmer covered for exactly 10 minutes. Stir the pilaf once or twice during cooking to make sure it does not stick to the base of the pan.

7   Once the pilaf has cooked for 10 minutes, remove from the heat, take off the lid and squeeze a little lemon juice over the mixture. Give it one last stir, then remove the bay leaf and lemon rind and discard. Allow the pilaf to stand in the pan for 2–3 minutes before serving.

8   Spoon the pilaf into a serving dish. Cut the hard-boiled eggs into wedges and arrange them attractively around the rice. Finally, sprinkle chopped scallions or chives and chopped cilantro over the pilaf to serve.

Swordfish in Caper & Tomato Sauce

*Swordfish has a wonderful meaty texture and its firmness makes
it ideal for baking, broiling or poaching. To depart from the usual
swordfish steaks, the recipe here offers an easy approach to preparing
this fish. The strident flavors of the tomatoes and capers complement
the milder taste of the fish. Serve this dish either hot or cold.*

1 First prepare the Tomato Sauce (see below), then place the whole piece
of fish, skin-side down, into the simmering sauce, cover and cook gently
for 40 minutes. Carefully turn the fish over halfway through cooking.
(It is advisable to use a fairly small, deep saucepan so that the sauce
covers most of the fish.)

2 Check the swordfish—if it is ready, the flesh in the middle of the fish will
be opaque and the whole of the flesh will be cooked through but not dry.

3 Add the capers and leave to rest for 5–10 minutes before serving. Slice
the swordfish thickly and serve with plenty of Tomato Sauce and a
generous sprinkling of chopped fresh parsley. This dish is very good
with a serving of Mashed Potatoes with Olive Oil (see page 72) and
a green vegetable.

1 recipe (3 cups) Tomato Sauce (see below)

2¼ pounds swordfish, in one piece with skin left on

3 tablespoons capers

Handful of chopped fresh parsley to garnish

Serves 6

TOMATO SAUCE

This recipe produces a delicious basic tomato sauce that can be served either
hot or cold with a large variety of dishes. The quantities given here make
about 3 cups, which serves approximately 6.

Heat 1 tablespoon of oil in a large saucepan over medium heat, then add
1 small onion, peeled and chopped. Soften the onion for a couple of minutes,
then add 2¼ pounds of chopped very ripe tomatoes, 2 peeled and crushed
cloves of garlic, 2 bay leaves, 2 chopped sticks of celery, 1 teaspoon of sugar
and some salt and freshly ground black pepper. Bring slowly to a boil and stew
gently for roughly 30 minutes until all the ingredients are well-cooked and
pulpy. Remove the bay leaves, then place the stewed tomato mixture in a food
processor and blend or pass through a sieve to remove the pips and skin.
Alternatively, if you do not have a food processor, pass the mixture through
a food mill. To serve hot, reheat the sauce very gently.

COLD SWORDFISH IN TOMATO CREAM

Once the swordfish is cooked, allow it to cool, then slice it thinly. Place the cold
tomato sauce in which the fish was cooked into a food processor and add ⅔ cup
of mayonnaise and 4 anchovy fillets. Process the mixture into a smooth cream.
If you are working without a blender, pass the tomato sauce through a sieve.
Then, pound the anchovies in a mortar with a pestle until finely crushed and
whisk into the tomato sauce with the mayonnaise and the capers. Pour the
sauce over the sliced fish, sprinkle with chopped fresh parsley and serve.

POACHED CHICKEN & VEGETABLES WITH RED & GREEN SAUCES

1 medium-sized chicken (4–5 pounds)

Vegetables for stock: 2 carrots, 1 onion, peeled, and 2 sticks celery, all chopped

2 bay leaves

Handful of fresh parsley sprigs

Salt to taste

6 peppercorns

4 medium-sized potatoes, peeled and chopped

4 medium-sized carrots, chopped

4 leeks, chopped

4 small zucchini

Serves 4

Simple, healthy poached chicken with vegetables can be transformed into something a little bit special with colorful red and green sauces (see right).

1   Place the whole chicken in a large pan that has a lid. Add the chopped stock vegetables, bay leaves, parsley sprigs, salt and peppercorns. Cover with water and bring slowly to a boil. Once the water is boiling, reduce the heat and simmer covered for approximately 1 hour or until the chicken is very tender.

2   Meanwhile, place the prepared potatoes, carrots and leeks in a large saucepan of boiling water. Cook for approximately 10 minutes until the vegetables are just softening, then add the zucchini and cook for a further 5 minutes until all the vegetables are cooked through and fairly soft.

3   Once everything is cooked, cut the chicken into 8 pieces and place it on a large, heated serving dish. Arrange the cooked vegetables around the chicken pieces. Serve with *Salsa Verde* and *Salsa Rossa* (see below). The stock made from the chicken can be reserved and used for other recipes, such as soups and risottos. Store it in a sealed container and keep in the refrigerator for 3 days or freeze for up to 3 months.

SALSA VERDE (GREEN SAUCE)

This is a sharp sauce made from capers and anchovies, which is ideal as an accompaniment to poached chicken or fish and meat dishes. The recipe given here serves 4–6.

Place 12 ounces of chopped fresh parsley, 1 small can of anchovies, 2 peeled and crushed cloves of garlic, 3 tablespoons of capers, 1 small onion, peeled and chopped and 4 tablespoons of white wine vinegar in a food processor and blend, or purée by hand in a mortar using a pestle. Trickle in 6 tablespoons of olive oil slowly and continue blending into a smooth but thickish sauce. If the sauce becomes too thick, add a little water.

SALSA ROSSA (RED SAUCE)

This piquant and spicy sauce made from red bell peppers and tomatoes can be used hot or cold to enhance any vegetable dish. This recipe serves 4–6.

Heat 3 tablespoons of olive oil in a saucepan and sauté 1 medium-sized onion, peeled and chopped, and 1 large red bell pepper, seeded and chopped. Cook gently until soft, but not brown, then add 4 chopped tomatoes and a pinch of salt and chili powder. Simmer covered for roughly 30 minutes until the vegetables are reduced to a pulp. Add a little water if necessary. Place the reduced pulp in a food processor and blend or pass through a sieve until the consistency is that of a thin purée.

CHICKEN BREASTS ROLLED WITH HAM & CHEESE

4 boneless, skinless chicken breast halves
(about 1½ pounds)

Salt and pepper to taste

4 slices of prosciutto or Serrano ham

4 "fingers" (1½ x ½ x ½ inches)
Gruyère cheese

3 tablespoons vegetable oil

1 tablespoon butter

1 small onion, peeled and chopped

⅔ cup dry white wine

1 tablespoon gluten-free Dijon mustard

1 tablespoon tomato purée

Serves 4

The ham and cheese rolled inside these flattened chicken breasts make an attractive spiral pattern when the chicken is sliced (see left). The dish can also be served cold and is delicious with a fresh green salad and a generous dollop of mayonnaise.

1 To prepare the chicken breasts, cut horizontally into each piece of meat three-quarters of the way, then open out the breasts.

2 Place each opened breast between two sheets of wax paper and, using a rolling pin, carefully pound them into thin, flat slabs of meat (or escalopes) of fairly even thickness. Avoid making holes in the meat. Remove the top sheets of paper and season the meat with salt and pepper.

3 Place a slice of prosciutto and a finger of Gruyère cheese on each escalope and carefully roll up each bundle into a neat curl. Tuck in the ends of the chicken and secure each roll with a piece of string to help it keep its shape.

4 Melt the butter and heat the oil in a heavy-based saucepan or skillet which has a lid. Cook the rolls in the fat, turning occasionally to brown them all over, then add the chopped onions. Once the onions have become translucent and the chicken rolls are browned, remove from the pan and keep warm on a heated plate covered with foil.

5 Deglaze the pan with the white wine (loosen the fat and the browned sediment at the bottom). Stir in the mustard and tomato purée and mix well. Return the chicken rolls to the pan and simmer covered for roughly 20 minutes. The chicken is cooked when the melted cheese begins to run out of the rolls.

6 Remove the chicken rolls from the sauce. Untie and discard the string. Slice each roll into 4–5 pieces, on a chopping board using a sharp knife. Arrange the slices attractively on a serving dish or on individual plates and pour the sauce around them. (If the sauce has reduced too much, add a little more wine and bring slowly to a boil to rescue it.) Serve with Potato Gratin (see page 72) or mashed potatoes and a green vegetable. If serving the dish cold—without the sauce—accompany with a green salad and a some Mayonnaise (see page 90).

CHICKEN BREASTS ROLLED WITH GOAT CHEESE AND HERBS
Flattened chicken breasts can also be rolled with goat cheese and a mixture of herbs. Prepare the chicken as above and mash ¼ pound of goat cheese with a bunch each of fresh shredded basil, chopped parsley, thyme and the juice of half a lemon. Spread the mixture on the escalopes and cook as above.

CHICKEN BREASTS STUFFED WITH RICOTTA

Chicken breasts are cooked in a wine and mustard sauce, then given richness with a melt-in-the-mouth ricotta and Parmesan stuffing.

1 Prepare the chicken breasts as for Chicken Breasts Rolled with Ham and Cheese (see opposite). Lay the chicken escalopes out on a chopping board and season with salt and pepper.

2 To make the stuffing, place all the ingredients in a mixing bowl and blend thoroughly using a fork.

3 Spread the ricotta mixture generously on to the chicken escalopes and carefully roll them up. Tuck in the ends and secure each roll with a piece of string. (This does not have to be done beautifully as the string will be removed later.)

4 Heat the oil and butter in a saucepan over medium heat and cook the rolled chicken pieces gently, turning occasionally to prevent them from becoming too brown.

5 Add the chopped onions, wine and mustard after roughly 10 minutes, then simmer gently for a further 20 minutes, turning the rolls from time to time. Once cooked, remove the chicken rolls from the sauce and allow to cool for 1–2 minutes. Remove the string and carefully slice each roll into 4–5 thick pieces using a very sharp knife. Place on a heated serving dish.

6 Stir the sauce remaining in the pan, adding a little more wine if there is too little moisture, or heating to reduce the liquid if it is too runny. (There should be roughly half the original quantity of liquid remaining.) Pour the sauce on to the rolled chicken slices, sprinkle with chopped fresh thyme or parsley and serve with Potato Soufflé (see page 73) and a green salad, or with Pesto Rice (see below).

FOR THE CHICKEN BREASTS

4 boneless, skinless chicken breast halves (about 1½ pounds)

Salt and pepper to taste

1 tablespoon olive oil and ½ tablespoon butter

1 small onion, peeled and chopped

⅔ cup dry white wine

1 tablespoon gluten-free Dijon mustard

2 teaspoons chopped fresh thyme or parsley to garnish

FOR THE RICOTTA STUFFING

1 cup ricotta cheese

3 tablespoons freshly grated Parmesan cheese

1 teaspoon dried thyme

1 large egg

Salt and pepper to taste

Serves 4

PESTO RICE

This aromatic and colorful rice dish is a delicious accompaniment to fish or chicken dishes. Served cold, it makes an ideal salad. This recipe serves 6.

Place 2 cups of short-grain risotto rice (such as Arborio) in a saucepan that has a lid and mix in ⅓ cup + 2 tablespoons of Pesto (see page 91). Make sure the grains are well coated in the pesto. Pour in 3 cups of boiling vegetable or chicken stock, add a little salt and stir. Bring to a boil, then reduce the heat and simmer covered for roughly 20 minutes. The rice should be *al dente*—or firm to bite—and quite dry. Carefully mix in another ⅓ cup + 2 tablespoons of pesto, 2 peeled and chopped shallots and the juice of 1 lemon. Adjust the seasoning and serve hot or cold with ¼ cup of freshly grated Parmesan cheese. Decorate the rice dish with a few shredded basil leaves.

SPICED BEEF STEW

3 tablespoons olive oil

2¼ pounds chuck or bottom round beef

3 cloves garlic, peeled and chopped

1 onion, peeled and chopped

1 teaspoon allspice

6 cloves

Freshly grated nutmeg to taste

1⅓ cups dark beer, such as Guinness or stout

½ pound (about 18) prunes, soaked and pitted

Salt and pepper to taste

2 teaspoons arrowroot

Serves 6–8

This warming winter dish can spice up any cold evening! The beef is cooked gently on the stove for a few hours, which allows the flavors of the spices and beer to be absorbed fully by the meat to create a robust and tasty stew.

1 Heat the oil over high heat in a large Dutch oven or other heavy-based pot that has a lid. Cut the beef into even-sized cubes and brown them rapidly in the heated oil. Reduce the heat and add the garlic, onion, allspice, cloves and nutmeg. Cook the meat for a few minutes until all the flavors are thoroughly blended together.

2 Pour in the beer and ½ cup water and slowly bring the stew to a boil. Then reduce the heat and add the prunes. Season the mixture with salt and pepper to taste. Cover the Dutch oven and simmer gently until the beef is very tender—this will take approximately 2–3 hours, depending on the quality of the beef used. Stir once or twice during cooking.

3 Once the meat has cooked, blend the arrowroot with 3 tablespoons of water and stir this into the Dutch oven. Bring the mixture back to a boil to thicken the sauce a little. Adjust the seasoning to taste. Serve the beef stew with either plain boiled rice or some mashed potatoes and a green vegetable.

BRAISED STEAK WITH MUSHROOMS

3 tablespoons olive oil

6 ounces smoked bacon, or uncooked ham, diced

1¼ pounds braising steak

8 shallots, peeled

½ pound button mushrooms

1⅓ cups red wine

1 tablespoon tomato purée

1 tablespoon gluten-free Dijon mustard

1 teaspoon dried thyme (or mixed herbs)

Salt and pepper to taste

Serves 4

This dish uses cheaper cuts of beef, such as chuck steak, which are tenderized in tasty juices during the slow cooking process.

1 Heat the oil over medium heat in a Dutch oven or other heavy-based pot that has a lid. Sauté the diced bacon (or ham) for 5 minutes, until crispy, then remove from the Dutch oven and set aside. Then brown the steak in the oil and bacon fat. Ensure that the meat is brown on both sides, then remove and set aside. Place the peeled shallots and mushrooms in the Dutch oven and brown them for approximately 5 minutes.

2 Pour the wine into the Dutch oven and bring to a boil. Add the tomato purée and the mustard and stir them in well. Sprinkle the dried thyme (or mixed herbs) over the mixture and season with salt and pepper. Place the steak back into the pan along with the bacon (or ham). Bring back to a boil, then simmer covered for approximately 2 hours until the meat is very tender. Turn the meat once during cooking.

3 When ready to serve, remove the steak, cut into 4 portions and place in a warmed serving dish. Reduce the sauce if it is too watery, then pour it over the steaks. Serve with plain boiled potatoes or mashed potatoes.

MARINATED BEEF WITH OLIVES

The beef is marinated in a sherry, herb and garlic mixture, then cooked with prosciutto and olives (see above). The success of this dish depends on the quality of the beef used. Top sirloin steak works well.

1 To prepare the marinade, mix together the olive oil, sherry, onion, garlic, herbs, salt and pepper in a large bowl.

2 Slice the beef into thin strips and place into the bowl with the marinade. Ensure each piece is well coated in the liquid. Cover and leave to marinate for at least 2 hours.

3 When ready to cook, heat the oil over high heat in a heavy-based pan and sauté the prosciutto for 1–2 minutes. Then, when the pan is very hot, remove the beef from the marinade and add to the pan. Sauté for 3–4 minutes only so the beef is not overcooked and tough. Turn the beef and prosciutto regularly during cooking to ensure that the strips are evenly cooked all over. Remove the pan from the heat.

4 Meanwhile, place the marinade in a small saucepan over high heat and boil it vigorously to reduce the liquid to half the original amount, then pour it into the pan containing the beef and ham. Add the olives and reheat quickly so as not to continue cooking the beef. Serve immediately, with plain boiled rice or potatoes.

FOR THE MARINADE

⅔ cup olive oil

6 tablespoons dry sherry

1 onion, peeled and chopped

2 cloves garlic, peeled and crushed

1 teaspoon chopped fresh thyme or oregano

Salt and pepper to taste

FOR THE BEEF

2¼ pounds top sirloin steak

Olive oil for frying

4 slices prosciutto or Serrano ham, cut into strips

15–20 green or black olives

Serves 6–8

STUFFED PEPPERS

Sweet red or green bell peppers are roasted with a tasty stuffing of rice, cooked ground meat, pine nuts and herbs. I particularly enjoy this dish when served with a fresh home-made tomato sauce.

Oil for greasing

2 cups cooked rice (leftover risotto is ideal) or ½ cup uncooked rice

1 tablespoon olive oil

1 small onion, peeled and chopped

2 cloves garlic, peeled and crushed

½ pound ground beef, lamb or pork

1 tomato, skinned and chopped

2 teaspoons chopped fresh parsley

1 teaspoon chopped fresh oregano or thyme

⅓ cup pine nuts

Salt and pepper to taste

2 large red bell peppers

2 tablespoons freshly grated Parmesan cheese

Serves 4

1   Preheat the oven to 350°F, 180°C, gas mark 4. Grease a medium-sized roasting pan with oil. If you have to cook the rice, place it in a saucepan with plenty of boiling water and cook for 12–15 minutes until *al dente*, or firm to bite. Drain and set aside.

2   Heat the oil in a skillet and cook the onion and garlic over low heat. Add the ground meat and cook for a further 10 minutes until the meat is browned and cooked through. (Cooked leftover ground meat may be used in place of raw meat, but should be cooked for only 1–2 minutes.) Add the tomato and herbs and cook for a further 2–3 minutes.

3   Add the cooked rice and stir well to ensure it absorbs the cooking juices. Mix in the pine nuts and season with salt and pepper. Stir well to combine all the ingredients, remove from the heat and allow to cool slightly.

4   Cut the peppers in half horizontally and remove all the seeds and pith. Spoon the stuffing into the peppers, pressing it in well to ensure all the crevices are filled.

5   Place the filled pepper halves into the roasting pan, ensuring they do not topple over, and cover with foil. Bake in the oven for 30 minutes. Remove the foil, sprinkle with the grated Parmesan cheese and bake uncovered for a further 30 minutes until the cheese is bubbling.

6   Serve the stuffed peppers with *Salsa Rossa* or Red Sauce (see page 56) or with fresh Tomato Sauce (see page 55) and a green salad.

STUFFED EGGPLANT

Eggplant can be stuffed in the same way as bell peppers. Cut them in half horizontally and scoop out as much flesh as possible without damaging the skins. Chop up some of the flesh and add it to the browned meat with the tomatoes and the herbs (see above). Fill the eggplant halves with the stuffing, pressing down firmly. Cook them as for the bell peppers above, sprinkling them with grated Parmesan cheese before the final 30 minutes of cooking.

STUFFED TOMATOES

Tomatoes, like the bell peppers and eggplant can also be stuffed with the ground meat, herbs and pine nut mixture, but need less cooking time. Cut the tops off fairly large, firm tomatoes. Scoop out the flesh and seeds and discard them (or use them when making a tomato sauce). Fill the empty shells with the stuffing mixture (see above), pressing it into the tomato shells firmly. Sprinkle with grated Parmesan cheese and bake uncovered for 30 minutes.

Meatballs in Tomato & Mushroom Sauce

Herbs, spices and a mixture of meats are combined in this unique recipe for juicy meatballs. A spicy mushroom and sherry sauce finishes the ensemble beautifully. This dish is equally good when made with ground lamb, but it is important that you buy meats of the best quality and have them finely minced so that they bind well during cooking.

1   Mix the ground beef and pork with the bacon, garlic, parsley, cumin and thyme in a bowl. Add the lemon juice and beaten egg and season with salt and pepper. Mix the ingredients together with your hands to ensure they are well blended. If you would like to test the seasoning, sauté some of the mixture in a little oil and taste. The meatballs should be quite spicy, but tailor them to suit your preferences.

2   Divide the meat mixture evenly and roll it into balls that are roughly the size of golf balls. Dampen your hands with a little water before rolling the mixture – this will prevent it from sticking to your hands.

3   Brown the meatballs in a Dutch oven or other heavy-based pot with the oil. Do this in small batches, to ensure they are all evenly cooked. Once browned, transfer the meatballs to a dish and keep warm in a low oven.

4   To make the sauce, heat the oil in the same Dutch oven or pot in which the meatballs were browned and soften the onion and garlic in the oil. Drain the mushrooms, reserving the soaking liquid, and chop them finely. Add them and the tomatoes to the pan. Cook for another minute or so.

5   Mix in the sherry, a little of the reserved mushroom soaking liquid, the bay leaf and the paprika. Slowly bring the sauce to a boil. Place the meatballs back into the pot with the sauce, season with salt and pepper and cover. Simmer gently for 30 minutes, turning the meatballs occasionally to ensure that they cook evenly and do not dry out. Once cooked, sprinkle with chopped parsley and serve with boiled rice, mashed potatoes or polenta (see page 46).

½ pound finely ground beef

½ pound finely ground pork

4 slices bacon, finely chopped

1 clove garlic, peeled and crushed

1 tablespoon chopped fresh parsley

1 teaspoon ground cumin

1 teaspoon dried thyme

Juice of 1 lemon

1 egg, beaten

Salt and pepper to taste

1 tablespoon olive oil

FOR THE SAUCE

1 tablespoon olive oil

1 medium-sized onion, peeled and chopped

1 clove garlic, peeled and crushed

¾ ounce dried mushrooms, soaked

3 tomatoes, peeled and chopped, or 8-ounce can of tomatoes

⅔ cup gluten-free dry sherry

1 bay leaf

1 tablespoon paprika

Salt and pepper to taste

Chopped fresh parsley to garnish

Serves 4–5

MEAT LOAF

The same ingredients used for the meatballs (see above) can be combined to make a meat loaf. Include 1 cup of cooked rice to lighten the texture a little. Instead of forming the meat mixture into balls, line a small loaf tin with slices of bacon and scoop the mixture into the tin, folding any excess bacon over the meat to surround it. Bake in the oven at 375°F, 190°C, gas mark 5 for about 1 hour until the meat is cooked. Drain the meat juices from the mould into a jug to use as gravy. Carefully turn out the loaf and slice. Serve hot with the gravy and a green vegetable. Meat loaf is also excellent cold, on its own with a salad or in sandwiches.

MOROCCAN LAMB

2 cloves garlic, peeled

1 teaspoon coarse salt

2 tablespoons chopped fresh rosemary

1 tablespoon cumin seeds

1 tablespoon coriander seeds

3 tablespoons olive oil

2 tablespoons paprika

1 teaspoon gluten-free cayenne pepper

1 boneless leg of lamb
(approximately 4½ pounds)

1 quart (4 cups) white wine

Serves 6

The spicy lamb is steamed in the oven for approximately 3 hours, which makes it very tender and succulent (see right).

1 Crush the garlic and salt together in a mortar with a pestle, adding the chopped rosemary, cumin seeds and coriander seeds gradually. Continue grinding until all of the ingredients are broken down. Add the olive oil, paprika and cayenne pepper and mix into a paste.

2 Place the lamb, cut-side up, on a large sheet of aluminum foil and work half of the spicy paste into it. Roll up the meat and secure with string. Rub the remaining paste on to the outside of the roll and wrap in foil. Leave for at least 3 hours or overnight (refrigerated) for the spices to flavor the meat.

3 Preheat the oven to 350°F, 180°C, gas mark 4. Unwrap the meat, leaving it tied, and place in a roasting pan. Pour the wine around it and cover with another sheet of foil. Seal the edges of the pan to prevent steam escaping.

4 Cook for 2 hours. Remove the foil, increase the heat to 400°F, 200°C, gas mark 6 and cook for another hour. If the pan juices dry out, add wine or water. To serve, remove the string, cut the meat into thick slices and place on a bed of Spicy Moroccan Rice (see page 68). Use the pan juices as gravy.

MOUSSAKA

3 medium-sized eggplants

Salt for dehydrating

4 tablespoons olive oil for frying, plus extra for greasing

1 onion, peeled and chopped

2 cloves garlic, peeled and crushed

2¼ pounds ground lamb

1½ tablespoons cornstarch

1 teaspoon thyme or oregano

Salt and pepper to taste

3 extra large eggs

1½ cups milk

1⅔ cups Tomato Sauce (see page 55)

Serves 4

This popular Greek dish is usually drenched in a béchamel sauce (made with wheat flour). This gluten-free version uses cornstarch.

1 Cut the eggplant into ½ inch-thick slices. Sprinkle with salt and set aside for 1 hour to draw out the juices. Preheat the oven to 350°F, 180°C, gas mark 4. Grease a deep rectangular 8 x 11-inch ovenproof dish. Heat the oil in a pan over medium heat, rinse the eggplant and pat dry, then sauté them for a few minutes until slightly browned. Remove and set aside.

2 Place the onion and garlic in the pan and sauté until transparent. Add the lamb and cook for 5 minutes until slightly browned. Mix in the cornstarch, herbs, salt and pepper and cook a little longer, then remove from the heat.

3 In a separate saucepan, beat the eggs with the milk, stirring and heating until thick, without allowing the mixture to boil. (Some people may like to add ½ cup grated cheese at this stage—I do not think it necessary.)

4 Arrange the ingredients in three layers in the ovenproof dish—first some eggplant, then the lamb, then the remaining eggplant. Pour over the tomato sauce and top with the egg and milk sauce. Place in the preheated oven for 1 hour or until the top is golden brown. Serve with a simple salad.

MARINATED & GRILLED LAMB KEBABS

Cut 1½ pounds of leg or shoulder fillet of lamb into 1-inch cubes. Make a marinade by mixing ⅓ cup of olive oil, the juice of 1 lemon, 4 peeled and crushed cloves of garlic, 1 tablespoon of chopped rosemary, 1 teaspoon of cumin and salt and pepper. Marinate the meat for about 1 hour. Remove from the marinade and thread on to skewers. Grill on a well-oiled rack, set 5–6 inches over glowing coals, for 4–6 minutes (medium-rare). Alternatively, broil the lamb on the rack of a broiler pan about 4 inches from the preheated broiler, for 4–6 minutes (medium-rare), turning occasionally. You can also thread some chopped red bell pepper, whole mushrooms or chopped onion on to the kebabs with the lamb.

MARINATED & GRILLED LAMB

I small boneless leg or shoulder of lamb (2–2½ pounds)

4 cloves garlic, peeled and sliced

I tablespoon dried rosemary

6 tablespoons olive oil

Juice of I lemon

I teaspoon ground cumin

Salt and pepper to taste

Serves 4

Lamb is tenderized in a marinade of olive oil, lemon, rosemary and garlic (see above). This dish is ideal for a special summer barbecue.

I Butterfly the boned lamb (open it out) and pierce the flesh with a sharp knife in several places. Push slivers of garlic and rosemary into the cuts. Prepare the marinade in a large bowl by mixing together the olive oil, lemon juice, ground cumin and salt and pepper. Place the meat into the marinade and mix to ensure it is well covered. Leave for at least 1 hour.

2 Remove the lamb from the marinade and place either on an oiled grill rack set 5–6 inches over glowing coals or under a broiler, about 4 inches from the heat. Cook for about 10 minutes on each side for medium-rare, brushing occasionally with the marinade.

BRAISED LAMB WITH EGGPLANT

The whole, boned leg of lamb is cooked in a casserole with eggplant, garlic and a mixture of spices. A thick sauce is made by blending the meat juices with the vegetables.

1. Slice the eggplant fairly thickly, sprinkle with salt and leave them to drain for at least 1 hour. This process will remove their bitter taste. Rinse and pat the slices dry.

2. Preheat the oven to 325°F, 160°C, gas mark 3. Heat the oil in a large ovenproof Dutch oven or other heavy-based pot with a lid and cook the lamb for 5–10 minutes until brown all over. Remove from the dish and keep warm. (The lamb does not need to be boned, but it does make the carving easier.)

3. In the same pot, cook over low heat without browning the chopped onion and garlic. Add the sliced eggplant and cook for a couple of minutes. Season with salt and pepper, sprinkle on the ground coriander and drop in the bay leaves.

4. Place the rolled lamb in the pot—lay it on top of the eggplant and onion with the join facing down. Pour in the stock and lemon juice and stir in the tomato purée. Bring the mixture to a boil, then cover tightly with a lid or aluminum foil.

5. Place the pot in the oven for 2 hours until the meat is very tender and the vegetables are very soft. Remove the aluminum foil covering, increase the oven temperature to 400°F, 200°C, gas mark 6, and cook for a further 15 minutes or so. This will brown the meat and improve its appearance.

6. Transfer the lamb to a serving dish and allow to rest in a warm place for 5–10 minutes, then remove the string. Meanwhile, put the vegetables and cooking juices into a bowl and mix with a hand-held blender to produce a thick sauce. Alternatively, pass the ingredients through a sieve. Place into a saucepan and reheat.

7. When the lamb is ready to serve, carve the meat into thick slices. Sprinkle with chopped fresh cilantro and serve the sauce separately. This dish is very good served with Fennel with Beans (see page 82) or plain boiled rice.

2 medium-sized eggplant

4 tablespoons olive oil

1 boneless leg of lamb, rolled

1 large onion, peeled and sliced

4 cloves garlic, peeled and chopped

Salt and pepper to taste

1 teaspoon ground coriander

2 bay leaves

2 cups chicken or beef stock

Juice of 1 lemon

1 tablespoon tomato purée

Chopped fresh cilantro to garnish

Serves 4–5

BRAISED LAMB CHOPS

Lamb chops can be braised in a similar way to the leg of lamb described in the recipe above. For 4 servings, use 8 lamb shoulder chops. Brown them on both sides and lay them on the eggplant. Follow the recipe above, but cook the lamb chops in the oven for a shorter time—approximately 1 hour—in only 1¼ cups of stock. This results in vegetables that are not as cooked as in the recipe above, so serve them whole, rather than puréed into a sauce.

PORK TENDERLOIN WITH APRICOTS

3 tablespoons olive oil

½ tablespoon butter

1 large pork tenderloin
(about 1½ pounds)

4 shallots, peeled and chopped

½ pound (about 30) ready-to-eat
dried apricots

1 bay leaf

1 teaspoon cinnamon

Salt and pepper to taste

1⅓ cups Port or Malaga wine

1⅓ cups beef stock

1 tablespoon gluten-free Dijon mustard

Serves 4

A unique sauce, flavored with apricots and sweet wine, is the secret of this dish, which is quick and easy to make.

1 Heat the oil and butter in a skillet that has a lid. Add the pork tenderloin and cook until brown all over. Remove, cut into 4 pieces and keep warm.

2 Now, sauté the shallots for 5 minutes, then add the apricots, bay leaf, cinnamon, salt, pepper, wine and stock. Bring to a boil, then simmer for 10 minutes, stirring occasionally, until the liquid has reduced to half the original quantity. Mix in the mustard.

3 Place the pork back in to the skillet and cook covered for 15 minutes, turning once. Remove the pork, place on to 4 plates, pour the sauce over each helping and serve with Spicy Moroccan Rice (see below).

SPICY MOROCCAN RICE

Wash 1¼ cups of Basmati rice and place it in 1⅔ cups of salted water. Bring to a boil and simmer for 10 minutes. Mix in 2 peeled and chopped shallots, ⅓ cup of seedless raisins, half a teaspoon each of ground coriander and ground cumin, a pinch of cayenne pepper, 1 tablespoon of olive oil and the juice of half a lemon. Leave to stand covered for 5 minutes to allow the flavors to permeate the rice.

PORK LOIN STUFFED WITH PÂTÉ

FOR THE PATE

½ pound pork liver, ground

½ pound (8–10) slices bacon,
finely chopped

¼ pound ham (about ½ cup),
finely chopped

1 clove garlic, peeled and crushed

1 small onion, peeled and finely chopped

1 teaspoon dried thyme

1 tablespoon brandy

Pinch of allspice

Salt and pepper to taste

Butter for greasing

When this dish is served, the center of each slice of pork is filled with a neat circle of liver, bacon and brandy pâté (see right)—an impressive detail that is ideal for special dinner parties. The trick is to freeze the pâté in a sausage shape, in order to stuff the pork loin with ease.

1 To make the pâté, blend the meats together. Add the remainder of the pâté ingredients and mix well. Leave to stand for roughly 1 hour to allow the flavors to infuse. To check the seasoning, fry a small amount of the mixture until cooked through, then allow to cool a little before tasting—it should be quite spicy. Adjust the seasoning if necessary.

2 Grease a sheet of aluminum foil that is roughly 12 inches long. Place the pâté mixture on to the foil and shape into a long sausage 12 inches long and roughly 1¾ inches in diameter. Wet your hands with a little water first, to prevent the pâté from sticking to them. Once you have formed the shape, roll the sausage using the foil. Place in the freezer until solid.

3 The pork loin should be stuffed with the frozen roll of pâté about 24 hours before it is cooked. To do this, make a cross-shaped incision through the center of each end of the meat using a long, sharp knife. Cut into the loin

from both ends, then push the frozen pâté roll through the opening in the meat to the other side, coaxing it gently where necessary. Mold the meat around the pâté roll to ensure that the pâté maintains its circular shape. Season the stuffed pork loin with salt and pepper and, if using fatless loin, wrap it in bacon slices. Wrap the meat in aluminum foil and set aside until the pâté has defrosted.

4   When ready to cook, preheat the oven to 350°F, 180°C, gas mark 4. Place the bacon-wrapped pork loin in a roasting pan with a little water around it (do not remove the foil). Bake in the preheated oven for roughly 2 hours. After this, remove the foil and increase the heat to 375°F, 190°C, gas mark 5. Roast the pork for approximately 1 more hour, until the pork is brown.

5   Take the pork out of the roasting pan and keep warm on a dish covered with aluminum foil. Now make a gravy by deglazing the roasting pan with the stock and mustard. Then boil vigorously for 1–2 minutes to reduce the liquid a little.

6   When ready to serve, cut the meat into fairly thick slices and pour some gravy over each portion. Serve with roast or boiled new potatoes and a vegetable purée.

FOR THE PORK LOIN & GRAVY

2¼ pounds boneless pork loin

8 slices bacon (if using fatless pork loin)

1 cup stock

1 tablespoon gluten-free Dijon mustard

Serves 6

4 Vegetable & Side Dishes

POTATO GRATIN

7 tablespoons butter, melted

2 pounds potatoes, peeled

Salt and pepper to taste

Freshly grated nutmeg to taste

2 cups milk

Serves 6

This mouthwatering dish is an ideal accompaniment to any grilled meat or fish.

1 Preheat the oven to 375°F, 190°C, gas mark 5. Brush a 8 x 12-inch gratin dish with a little of the melted butter.

2 Finely slice the peeled potatoes, using a mandolin, if possible. Arrange the sliced potatoes in layers in the gratin dish—brush each layer with melted butter, then season with salt, pepper and a little freshly grated nutmeg before arranging the next layer on top. Continue in this way until the potato slices are all used, ensuring you do not fill the dish right up to the top, so that the milk does not boil over during cooking.

3 Before you brush the last potato layer with melted butter, pour the milk into the dish up to a level just below the top layer of potatoes. Brush on the remaining melted butter and season with salt, pepper and grated nutmeg.

4 Cover the gratin with foil and place in the preheated oven for 45 minutes. Remove the foil and return to the oven for another 45 minutes, until the top of the gratin is brown and crispy and the potatoes are cooked through.

POTATO GRATIN VARIATIONS

If you would prefer this dish to be less rich, substitute vegetable or chicken stock for the milk. To make the dish more creamy, replace some of the milk with light or heavy cream.

Include thinly peeled and sliced onions or freshly grated cheese between the potato layers for additional flavor, or top the entire dish with freshly grated Parmesan cheese.

Another variation for potato gratin is to flavor the melted butter with garlic and mixed dried herbs—simply crush a clove of garlic into the butter and sprinkle with some herbs.

MASHED POTATOES WITH OLIVE OIL

2 pounds potatoes, peeled and cut

¾ cup hot milk

4 tablespoons extra virgin olive oil

Salt and pepper to taste

Serves 6

Substituting olive oil for butter produces a highly flavorful mashed potato that is ideal for serving with braised and grilled meat.

Boil the peeled and cut potatoes in a large saucepan for 10–15 minutes, until soft. Drain thoroughly, then return them to the pan. Mash the potatoes while pouring in the hot milk a little at a time, until all the milk is used up and the mashed potato is creamy; more hot milk can be added if necessary. Add the oil and season with salt and pepper.

POTATO SOUFFLÉ

The addition of mashed potato to a basic soufflé results in a tasty and substantial side dish that is great served with grilled fish.

1 Preheat the oven to 350°F, 180°C, gas mark 4. Lightly grease a 6-cup soufflé dish with melted butter.

2 Peel and chop the potatoes and boil for 10–15 minutes, until soft. Drain thoroughly, then mash until creamy.

3 Add the egg yolks, butter, cream, salt and pepper and a little grated nutmeg over the dish. Mix the ingredients together thoroughly.

4 Beat the egg whites until stiff and fairly dry and then fold into the potatoes. Pour the potato mixture into the greased soufflé dish and bake in the preheated oven for 45 minutes until the center is set. Shake the dish gently—if the center wobbles just slightly, it is set; if it wobbles dramatically, return the soufflé to the oven for a little longer.

2¼ pounds potatoes

5 large eggs, separated

7 tablespoons butter, plus extra for greasing

½ cup light cream

Salt and pepper to taste

Freshly grated nutmeg to taste

Serves 6

SPICY POTATOES IN TOMATO SAUCE

In this side dish, chunky potato wedges are cooked in a fresh tomato sauce that is flavored with a delicious blend of herbs and spices. Make the sauce as mild or as fiery as suits your own taste. Serve the dish with grilled meats.

1 Peel the potatoes and cut them into ¾-inch cubes. Heat the oil in a heavy-based pan and sauté the potatoes for 10–15 minutes until cooked through and brown on the outside.

2 Add the chopped garlic, vinegar, paprika, ground cumin, oregano and chili powder and cook for a minute or two, stirring well to blend all the flavors thoroughly.

3 Add the tomato sauce—fresh sauce is ideal (see page 55), but any of the canned or bottled varieties may also be used. Heat the dish through until the sauce is bubbling nicely. Serve with a generous sprinkling of chopped fresh parsley.

1¼ pounds potatoes

Oil for frying

1 clove garlic, peeled and chopped

1 tablespoon red wine vinegar

1 tablespoon paprika

1 teaspoon ground cumin

1 teaspoon dried oregano

Pinch of chili powder (or to taste)

1½ cups fresh Tomato Sauce (see page 55), or canned or bottled

Chopped fresh parsley to garnish

Serves 4–6

SPICY SWEET POTATOES
An interesting variation on this recipe is to use sweet potatoes instead of the ordinary ones. The sweetness contrasts well with the spicy tomato sauce. Pesto (see page 90) is also delicious with sautéed potatoes of any kind.

RÖSTI

1¼ pounds potatoes

½ tablespoon butter

1 tablespoon olive oil

Salt and pepper to taste

Serves 4

Made without any flour or eggs to bind it (see inset, right), this potato cake is excellent to serve with roasted or grilled meat.

1 Parboil the potatoes in their skins for 10 minutes. Drain and set aside to cool. Peel the potatoes and grate them using a coarse grater—this is easier to do if they are chilled beforehand.

2 Heat the butter and oil in a 8-inch non-stick skillet. Spread the grated potatoes evenly in the pan, patting them down firmly. Reduce the heat to a low setting, season with salt and pepper and cook for 10 minutes.

3 Turn the rösti over to brown the other side. To do this, place a plate over the pan and turn the potato cake out on to it, then quickly slide it back into the pan. (Add a touch more oil at this point if the pan looks dry.) Cook the second side for 10 minutes then divide the rösti into 4 equal portions and serve. You may find that the rösti refuses to hold together, but this does not matter as it will be delicious anyhow.

VARIATIONS ON ROSTI

Individual rösti can also be made by forming a few small patties rather than one large one with the grated potatoes. Mold them in the palm of your hand, pressing the potato mixture together firmly, then fry them in plenty of oil for roughly 5 minutes on each side.

Flavorings can be added to the grated potato mixture, but do bear in mind that these should be fairly strong flavors in small quantities, as there is nothing except the natural potato starch to act as a binder. Adding a few chopped anchovy fillets to the grated potato makes a delicious fish cake. Some grated onion or fresh Parmesan cheese also makes an interesting addition and any herb will give the rösti an aromatic flavor.

ROAST POTATOES WITH ROSEMARY & GARLIC

1¼ pounds potatoes

6 tablespoons olive oil

Salt and black pepper to taste

2 tablespoons rosemary leaves, chopped

2 cloves garlic, peeled and chopped

Serves 4–6

1 Preheat the oven to 425°F, 220°C, gas mark 7. Peel the potatoes and then cut them into ¾-inch cubes. Place them in a large saucepan of salted water and parboil them for 5 minutes, then drain.

2 Pour the oil into a large roasting pan and heat it on the stove top. Add the potatoes, turning them to ensure they are well coated in oil. Season with salt and plenty of freshly ground black pepper. Sprinkle chopped rosemary and garlic over the potatoes and place the pan in the top half of the oven for 30 minutes until they are brown and crispy all over (see right), turning them once or twice during cooking.

MUSHROOMS WITH LEMON & THYME

½ pound oyster or button mushrooms, brushed clean of dirt

2 tablespoons extra virgin olive oil

2 cloves garlic, peeled and crushed

Several sprigs fresh thyme

Juice of I lemon

Salt and black pepper to taste

Serves 4

This delicious concoction of mushrooms sautéed with garlic, lemon juice and fresh thyme (see above) can be served either as an appetizer or as part of an entrée with grilled meat or fish.

I   Clean and trim the mushrooms and slice any that seem too large. Heat the oil in a shallow saucepan and, when hot, add the crushed garlic, the fresh thyme leaves (removed from their stalks) and the lemon juice. Cook for 2–4 minutes over medium heat.

2   Add the mushrooms to the pan and sauté gently for 15 minutes until cooked through. Season with salt and plenty of freshly ground black pepper. Remove from the pan and serve either hot or cold in individual terracotta dishes sprinkled with fresh thyme leaves.

MUSHROOMS WITH PROSCIUTTO AND CHILI
Heat 2 tablespoons of olive oil and 2 tablespoons of butter in a skillet. Add 6 chopped shallots and 1 crushed clove of garlic and cook for 5 minutes. Mix in ½ pound of button mushrooms and cook for a further 3 minutes. Stir in 1 ounce of chopped prosciutto, half a teaspoon of chili powder, 6 tablespoons of water and 1 teaspoon of lemon juice and cook over high heat until the liquid has almost evaporated. Add ⅓ cup of red wine and cook until the liquid is reduced. Stir in another crushed clove of garlic and sprinkle with chopped fresh parsley.

MUSHROOMS STUFFED WITH PARMESAN CHEESE

These baked mushrooms, stuffed with garlic, herbs and cheese make an attractive appetizer or side dish.

1 Preheat the oven to 375°F, 190°C, gas mark 5. Wash the mushrooms, then remove the stalks. Set aside the caps and chop the stalks finely.

2 Mix the chopped stalks, garlic, parsley and Parmesan cheese with the olive oil. Add freshly ground black pepper, but not salt as the cheese is salty.

3 Brush the mushroom caps with olive oil and sit them in a baking pan or on a roasting pan. Divide the stuffing and spoon it into the mushroom caps. Cook in the preheated oven for 20 minutes. Remove from the oven, sprinkle with more fresh parsley, and allow to cool a little to serve.

4 large, flat mushrooms

2 cloves garlic, peeled and crushed

Handful of chopped fresh parsley

¼ cup freshly grated Parmesan cheese

2 tablespoons olive oil, plus extra for brushing

Freshly ground black pepper to taste

Serves 4

VEGETABLE-STUFFED MUSHROOMS

Make a vegetable purée using 4 ounces of a vegetable of your choice. Finely chop 2 shallots and fry until translucent. Remove from the heat and mix with the purée. Add ground coriander and salt and pepper to taste. Spread a tablespoon of purée on to each mushroom cap (prepared as above). Cook as above. Sprinkle with chopped fresh cilantro to serve.

BLACK-EYED PEAS WITH MUSHROOMS

The smoky flavor of black-eyed peas contrasts wonderfully with the earthy taste of mushrooms in this delicious side dish.

1 It is not necessary to soak black-eyed peas before cooking. Boil the peas for 45 minutes, until tender. If desired, add a couple of bay leaves and a chopped onion to the water for extra flavor, but do not add salt. Once cooked, drain the beans and discard the bay leaves and onion.

2 Meanwhile, wash and trim the mushrooms and cut them into small pieces, if large. Heat the oil in a skillet and add the mushrooms and garlic. Cook for 5 minutes, then add the lemon juice.

3 Remove the pan from the heat, add the cooked beans and mix well. Season the mushroom and bean mixture liberally with salt and plenty of freshly ground black pepper. Drizzle with a little olive oil and sprinkle with chopped fresh cilantro to serve. This dish is also delicious if mixed with rice—use 2½ cups cooked rice for this recipe.

½ pound (1¼ cups) black-eyed peas

2 bay leaves (optional)

1 onion, peeled and chopped (optional)

½ pound mushrooms (cremini are good but any variety will do)

3 tablespoons olive oil

2 cloves garlic, peeled and crushed

Juice of 1 lemon

Salt and black pepper to taste

Chopped fresh cilantro to garnish

Serves 4–6

ROASTED VEGETABLES

Roasting vegetables with garlic and olive oil gives them a distinct flavor and brings out the sweetness of red and yellow bell peppers; try them as a meal or a side dish to serve with roasts and grills.

1 red and 1 yellow bell pepper
1 large eggplant
2 small zucchini
Salt for dehydrating
1 fennel bulb
1 large onion, peeled
2 firm tomatoes
2 cloves garlic, peeled and crushed
⅓ cup olive oil
Salt and black pepper to taste
Shredded fresh basil to garnish
Serves 4–6

1 Chop the bell peppers into 1–1¼-inch squares. Cut the eggplant and zucchini into 1–1¼-inch cubes. Toss the eggplant in salt. Allow to stand for an hour or so to draw out the bitter juices, then rinse the cubes and pat them dry with paper towel.

2 Preheat the oven to 475°F, 240°C, gas mark 9. Rinse the fennel and trim the root end. Cut off the stalks and feathery leaves, remove any bruised outer stalks, then slice the root into 1–1¼-inch cubes. Chop the onion and quarter the tomatoes.

3 Arrange all the vegetables on a shallow roasting pan and sprinkle with the crushed garlic. Toss all the vegetables in the oil, making sure they are all well coated and season liberally with salt and pepper.

4 Place the roasting pan in the top part the oven and roast for 30 minutes. Turn all the vegetables once during cooking. When done, they should be toasted and brown on the edges, but not overcooked. Serve either hot or cold with plenty of shredded basil leaves to decorate.

ROASTED EGGPLANT AND SWEET POTATO WITH SPINACH
Place 1 chopped eggplant in a bowl and stir in 2 tablespoons of olive oil. Add a pinch of cayenne pepper, a sprinkling of black pepper and half a tablespoon of lemon juice. Pour into a roasting pan with 1 chopped red bell pepper. Place 1 chopped and peeled sweet potato and a 15-ounce can of chickpeas in the bowl and add half a tablespoon of olive oil, half a tablespoon of lemon juice, a pinch of paprika and a little freshly grated nutmeg. Stir to blend, then place in the roasting pan. Cook the vegetables in the oven at 475°F, 240°C, gas mark 9 for 30 minutes, then mix in 2 ounces (about ¾ cup) uncooked shredded spinach. Season with black pepper to taste. If the dish is too dry, add more olive oil or lemon juice. Serve with yogurt mixed with chopped mint.

ROASTED FENNEL
Trim 3 large bulbs of fennel and cut each into 6 wedges. Place the fennel in a mixing bowl and toss with 1 tablespoon of olive oil and plenty of salt and freshly ground black pepper. Place on a baking sheet and cook in the oven at 475°F, 240°C, gas mark 9 for 1 hour until browned at the edges and tender.

ROASTED CARROTS AND PARSNIPS
Chop 1 pound each of peeled carrots and peeled parsnips into 1-inch pieces. Mix with ½ pound of peeled shallots and toss the vegetables in 1 tablespoon of olive oil, a pinch of dried thyme, a little salt and some freshly ground black pepper. Roast in the oven at 475°F, 240°C, gas mark 9 for 1 hour until tender.

ROASTED PEPPER SALAD

Roasted peppers are so tasty that very little additional flavoring is needed. This dish is a good light first course (see right) and can be used as an accompaniment to many dishes, such as grilled or roasted meat or fish. I suggest red or yellow bell peppers, as these are easier to peel and attractively colored.

1 Preheat the oven to 475°F, 240°C, gas mark 9. Brush the bell peppers with a little olive oil and place them in the top half of the oven. Cook for 20–30 minutes, turning the vegetables once, until the skins are blackened and blistered and the flesh is soft.

2 Remove the bell peppers from the oven and place them into a plastic freezer bag. Seal the bag immediately and allow the peppers to stand for 15 minutes, to loosen the skins.

3 Carefully peel the peppers, cut off the stem and scrape out the seeds, taking care not to damage the flesh. Cut the flesh into strips, place in a serving dish and drizzle lightly with olive oil. Season with salt and freshly ground pepper to taste and sprinkle with some chopped fresh cilantro. Serve immediately.

4 large red bell peppers or yellow bell peppers (or a mixture of both)

Olive oil for brushing

Salt and black pepper to taste

Chopped fresh cilantro to garnish

Serves 4–6

FRIED PEPPERS

Long and slim, Italian frying peppers are best for this recipe (see right), in which they are pan-fried whole in olive oil and salt.

Heat the oil in a large skillet over medium heat and cook the peppers whole, including the stems, for about 15 minutes, turning them from time to time. Do not overcook them – they are done when they become a little floppy and brown in places. Sprinkle with plenty of freshly ground sea salt and serve either hot or cold with grilled meat or fish.

⅓ cup olive oil

12 Italian frying peppers

Freshly ground sea salt to taste

Serves 4–6

PEPPER, TOMATO AND ANCHOVY RELISH

This relish is based on green bell peppers and makes an ideal accompaniment to grilled meats. Chop 4 seeded green bell peppers into strips and cut these into roughly ½-inch pieces. Chop 1–2 chilies and peel and chop 2 cloves of garlic. Skin and chop 4 medium-sized tomatoes and roughly chop 4 canned anchovy fillets. Heat 6 tablespoons of olive oil in a saucepan over medium heat, then add the peppers, chilies, garlic and chopped anchovies. Cook for about 5 minutes, stirring constantly to ensure that none of the ingredients stick to the pan or burn. Add the peeled and chopped tomatoes and allow the mixture to stew for roughly 10 minutes until the tomatoes have reduced to a pulp. Add salt if necessary. Serve sprinkled with chopped fresh parsley.

FENNEL WITH CHEESE SAUCE

This combination of sweet, scented fennel topped with a rich cheese sauce is delightful.

2 fennel bulbs

½ tablespoon butter

1⅓ cups Cheese Sauce (see page 91)

Serves 4

1 Rinse the fennel and trim the root end. Cut off the stalks and feathery leaves, remove any bruised outer stalks and cut the fennel into quarters. Place in a large saucepan with the butter and 2–3 tablespoons of water. Cover the pan tightly and cook over low heat for 20 minutes, turning once, until just tender—do not overcook them. Add a little more water to the pan if necessary.

2 Transfer the cooked fennel to a warm serving dish (terracotta dishes are ideal for gratins) and pour over the Cheese Sauce (see page 91). Place under a broiler for 10 minutes, then sprinkle with fronds of fennel to serve.

LEEK OR CAULIFLOWER WITH CHEESE SAUCE

Use cheese sauce with leeks or cauliflower in the same way as with fennel. With leeks, cut off the roots and trim the tops. Cut each leek in half lengthways to within 1½ inches of the root ends. Separate the leaves and wash them thoroughly under running cold water. Cook in a large saucepan with a small amount of water for 10 minutes, until soft. Pour over the cheese sauce to serve.

Cauliflower can be cooked whole in a large covered saucepan with boiling water for 15–20 minutes until soft. Serve the cauliflower whole with the cheese sauce poured over the top.

ZUCCHINI & SESAME GRATIN

Sesame has a wonderful nutty flavor that, combined with melted cheese, enlivens the taste of zucchini in this warming side dish. Serve it with meat dishes.

1   Wash and trim the zucchini then cut them into ½-inch-thick slices. Heat the sesame oil in a skillet over low heat, then add the chopped garlic and sliced zucchini. Sauté gently for 5–6 minutes, turning the zucchini occasionally to cook them on both sides. Make sure you do not overcook them—they should remain *al dente,* or firm to bite. Add salt and freshly ground black pepper.

2   Place the cooked zucchini in a flameproof dish. Cover them with the grated cheese and sprinkle with the sesame seeds.

3   Broil the zucchini and cheese until the cheese begins to melt and sizzle and the seeds are slightly toasted—about 2–3 minutes. Ensure that you do not burn the topping.

1 pound zucchini

1½ tablespoons sesame oil

4 cloves garlic, peeled and chopped

Salt and black pepper to taste

1 cup cheddar cheese, coarsely grated

1 tablespoon sesame seeds

Serves 4

EGGPLANT GRATIN

Baked eggplant and tomatoes are given a golden melted cheese topping. Make sure you use cheese that melts properly when heated. Goat cheese is best, due to its fairly strong flavor, but Mozzarella, Fontina or a mild Cheddar are also good.

1   Cut the eggplant into ½-inch-thick slices. Sprinkle with salt and leave for 1 hour to draw out the bitter juices. (This process also ensures that the eggplant absorb less oil when fried.) Rinse the slices and pat dry with a sheet of paper towel. Preheat the oven to 400°F, 200°C, gas mark 6.

2   Heat the oil in a skillet and add the eggplant, a few slices at a time. Sauté them quickly, turning them over during cooking to ensure that they are cooked through.

3   Grease a shallow ovenproof dish thoroughly with a little oil and arrange the slices of sautéed eggplant in the base of the dish in alternate layers with the peeled and thickly sliced tomatoes. Sprinkle on salt, pepper and a little of the oregano between each layer. Continue to layer the vegetables until all the ingredients are used up or until the dish is full.

4   Cover the eggplant and tomatoes with a layer of the cheese slices and place the dish in the preheated oven. Bake for 30 minutes until the cheese has melted and is bubbling and the eggplant and tomatoes are piping hot. Remove the Eggplant Gratin from the oven and serve immediately with a tossed green salad.

4 large eggplant

Salt for dehydrating

3 tablespoons olive oil, plus extra for greasing

2 large tomatoes, peeled and thickly sliced

Salt and pepper to taste

2 teaspoons dried oregano

10 ounces cheese, thinly sliced

Serves 4

GREEN BEANS WITH GARLIC & ALMONDS

Green beans fried in garlic and olive oil are topped with toasted almonds in this tasty side dish.

I pound green beans

½ cup slivered almonds

3 tablespoons olive oil

4 cloves garlic, peeled and sliced

Salt and freshly ground black pepper to taste

Serves 4

1 Preheat the oven to 350°F, 180°C, gas mark 4. Top and tail the beans (and string them, if necessary) and cut each bean into 2–3 pieces. Drop them into a saucepan of boiling, salted water and cook until slightly tender. This will take roughly 5 minutes, but the cooking time does depend on the type of bean used. Do not overcook them—they should not be soft, but should retain some bite. Once cooked, drain the beans and set aside.

2 Toast the almonds by placing them on a baking sheet and cooking them in the preheated oven for 8–10 minutes until they turn light brown in color. Stir occasionally during cooking to ensure the nuts color evenly.

3 Heat the oil in a saucepan and sauté the garlic over medium heat for a few minutes until the slices begin to brown. Remove from the heat and add the cooked beans, tossing them around the pan to ensure they are coated in oil and garlic. Season with salt and plenty of freshly ground black pepper. Sprinkle the almonds over the beans to serve.

GREEN BEANS WITH HAZELNUTS

Replace the almonds in the recipe above with roasted hazelnuts that have been fried in butter for 3 minutes. Mix them with 1 teaspoon of grated lemon rind and a pinch of cayenne pepper.

FENNEL WITH BEANS

I suggest navy beans for this recipe, but pinto beans are just as suitable. The soft-textured beans and crisp fennel contrast well.

½ pound (about 1–1⅓ cups) dried navy beans, or a 15-ounce can, rinsed and drained

I fennel bulb

3 tablespoons olive oil

I clove garlic, crushed

½ teaspoon cumin seeds

Salt and pepper to taste

Juice of ½ lemon to serve

Serves 4

1 If using dried beans, soak them overnight, then cook them as described on page 87. Otherwise, use canned, ready-cooked beans. Rinse and trim the fennel bulb, cut it in half and slice thinly. Heat the oil in a skillet which has a lid and cook the fennel and garlic over low heat for 5 minutes.

2 Add the cooked beans and the cumin seeds. Season with salt and pepper and cook covered for a further 10 minutes, stirring occasionally.

3 When ready to serve, squeeze the lemon juice over the beans and fennel and decorate with fennel fronds if you have any. This dish is very good with pork or ham and perfect served with Braised Lamb and Eggplant (see page 67).

FAVA BEANS & HAM

This protein-packed side dish also makes a hearty first course. It looks attractively rustic served in individual terra cotta dishes (see below).

1 Shell the beans and place them in a saucepan of salted boiling water. Cook for 5–10 minutes until tender. (The cooking time for fava beans depends entirely on their size—the larger they are, the longer they take.) Ensure you do not overcook them. Drain and set aside. If using large beans, remove the skin from each bean once cooked.

2 Heat the oil in a saucepan and gently sauté the scallions for 1–2 minutes until they begin to soften.

3 Add the strips of prosciutto or ham to the pan with the scallions and cook for 2–3 minutes, stirring constantly, then add the beans. Season with freshly ground black pepper and a little salt if necessary (the prosciutto may be fairly salty itself) and cook for a few more minutes, stirring constantly, until the beans and ham are cooked. When ready to serve, divide the beans into 4 terra cotta dishes and sprinkle with the parsley.

2 pounds fava beans
3 tablespoons olive oil
3–4 scallions, chopped
¼ pound prosciutto or Serrano ham, cut into strips
Salt and black pepper to taste
1 tablespoon chopped fresh parsley to garnish, optional
Serves 4

FAVA BEAN SALAD

Small and tender fava beans that have been skinned and cooked make a tasty and filling salad on their own. Simply toss them in Vinaigrette (see page 91) and serve on lettuce leaves.

CHICKPEAS WITH SPINACH

1 pound fresh spinach (½ pound frozen spinach may be used)

6 tablespoons olive oil

4 cloves garlic, peeled and crushed

15-ounce can chickpeas, rinsed and drained

1 teaspoon ground cumin

1 teaspoon gluten-free paprika

Juice of 1 lemon

Salt and pepper to taste

Serves 4–6

The nutty texture of chickpeas and the softness of spinach purée in this recipe (see above) is a remarkably successful combination. In Spain, the dish is served as tapas or as an appetizer. It is great with grilled fish.

1 If using fresh spinach, wash thoroughly and place in a large saucepan with only the water that clings to the leaves. Cook over low heat until the leaves start to wilt. (Cook frozen spinach according to packet instructions.) Drain thoroughly, squeezing out excess water, then chop finely.

2 Heat the oil in an open saucepan and gently sauté the garlic for a couple of minutes until golden brown.

3 Add the chickpeas to the pan with the garlic, then add the cumin, paprika, lemon juice, salt, pepper and spinach. Simmer over low heat for roughly 20–30 minutes, stirring occasionally, until the spinach is reduced to a pulp. Adjust the seasoning and serve immediately.

COOKING LEGUMES

Legumes are very important ingredients in a gluten-free diet—besides being excellent sources of fiber, their uses in cooking are countless. There is also a huge range of choice with dried beans, peas and lentils.

Most dried beans should be soaked overnight, then cooked in plenty of boiling water which can be flavored with a clove-studded onion or a bay leaf or two. However, never flavor the water with salt—this toughens the skins, as does any acidity such as tomato sauce or lemon juice.

It is important to fast-boil beans for at least 10 minutes at the beginning of cooking to remove the toxins. Then simmer the beans until cooked. The time taken to cook beans varies according to variety. It is worth experimenting with precooked, canned beans, as they are readily available, save time and can be just as tasty.

VEGETABLE "SPAGHETTI"

This pretty side dish is an attractive and tasty accompaniment to almost any meal and makes a great alternative to the usual rice or potatoes.

1 Cut the vegetables into thin strips (julienne). Heat the oil in a wok or a skillet, add the garlic, carrots and turnips and stir-fry for 3–4 minutes. Add the remaining vegetables and fry for a further 3–4 minutes until the vegetables are *al dente*, or firm to bite. Season with salt and pepper.

2 Place in a serving dish, then sprinkle with grated Parmesan cheese and decorate with shredded basil leaves to serve.

1 pound mixture of carrots, zucchini, peppers, turnips, leeks and garlic

3 tablespoons olive oil

Salt and pepper to taste

Freshly grated Parmesan cheese to serve

A few leaves shredded fresh basil to serve

Serves 4–6

CARROTS WITH CUMIN

The flavors of cumin and carrots are successfully combined in this side dish, which is good served with lamb or pork.

1 Place the carrots in a saucepan with the stock. Bring to a boil, then simmer covered for 5 minutes, stirring once or twice, until *al dente*, or firm to bite.

2 Remove from the heat and drain any remaining liquid. Pour in the olive oil, add the cumin seeds and mix well. Season with freshly ground black pepper and some salt, if necessary—the stock may be salty enough in itself.

1 pound carrots, washed and sliced into thin strips (julienne) or ¼-inch rounds

½ cup concentrated chicken stock (1 gluten-free stock cube or home-made stock)

1 tablespoon olive oil

2 tablespoons cumin seeds

Salt and pepper to taste

Serves 4–5

CARROTS WITH MANGO CHUTNEY

Another appetizing way to serve carrots is to cook them in stock as above, then, instead of adding cumin and oil, add 2 tablespoons of mango chutney. This produces a sweet-and-sour flavor that is perfect for pork dishes.

Tomato & Artichoke Salad

2 pounds baby globe artichokes (or canned artichoke hearts)

4 tomatoes, medium-sized, firm but ripe

Balsamic Vinaigrette (see page 48) to taste

Salt and pepper to taste

Handful of chopped fresh parsley to serve

Serves 4–6

Tomatoes and artichokes are combined with a balsamic vinaigrette to make a refreshing summer salad that is ideal with broiled fish.

1 If using fresh baby globe artichokes, remove 2–3 rows of the tough outer leaves of each artichoke, then trim the stalk and cut off the cone-shaped tip to remove the tough pointed ends. Bring a saucepan of salted water to a boil, add the artichokes and boil for 10 minutes until tender. Drain and allow them to cool, then cut each artichoke in half and place in a mixing bowl. (Canned artichoke hearts are precooked, so can be halved without any preparation.)

2 Cut the tomatoes into wedges and place in the bowl with the artichoke hearts. Prepare the Balsamic Vinaigrette (see page 48) and pour it into the bowl, tossing the salad to ensure that the tomatoes and artichokes are all well coated in the dressing. Season with salt and pepper. To serve, sprinkle with chopped fresh parsley.

Tomatoes Stuffed with Herb Rice

4 medium-sized tomatoes, firm but ripe

1 cup cooked rice of any kind

2 tablespoons mixed fresh herbs (chives, basil, parsley, tarragon), chopped

1 shallot, peeled and chopped

1 tablespoon olive oil

1 egg, hard-boiled, chopped

Juice of 1 lemon

Salt and pepper to taste

Chopped fresh parsley to garnish

Serves 4

Aromatic herb rice makes a perfect stuffing for tomato shells. Make sure you select tomatoes that are firm, but ripe, so that the skins are tough enough to hold their shape, yet have good flavor. This side dish is also good as an appetizer.

1 Cut the tops off the tomatoes and carefully scoop out the seeds and pulp using a spoon, leaving the tomato shell empty and intact.

2 Place the rice in a bowl and mix in the fresh herbs. Add the shallot, olive oil, hard-boiled egg, lemon, salt and pepper and stir until all the ingredients are blended. Season the insides of the tomato shells and fill with the stuffing. Garnish with chopped fresh parsley to serve.

TOMATOES STUFFED WITH TUNA

Prepare 4 medium-sized tomatoes as for Tomatoes Stuffed with Herb Rice, above. Drain and mash one 6-ounce can of tuna fish with 2 tablespoons of mayonnaise, using a fork. Mix in 1 tablespoon of chopped gherkins, 1 tablespoon of chopped celery and 1 peeled and chopped shallot. Season with plenty of freshly ground black pepper and some salt, if the fish is not salty enough itself. Season the insides of the tomato shells also before stuffing them with the tuna mayonnaise. Decorate the stuffed tomatoes with a small sprig of fresh parsley. Allow 1 tomato per serving.

TOMATOES BAKED WITH PARMESAN CHEESE

This tasty cheese and tomato snack (see above) can be served either hot or cold and makes an excellent accompaniment to almost any dish, particularly soups.

1 Preheat the oven to 425°F, 220°C, gas mark 7. Grease a medium-sized baking pan thoroughly with a little olive oil. Slice the tomatoes thickly using a sharp knife and lay them out on the greased baking pan.

2 Make a paste by mixing together the grated Parmesan cheese, olive oil and chopped parsley. Season the paste with freshly ground black pepper (salt is not necessary as the cheese is quite salty itself). Spread a little of the cheese paste on to each slice of tomato and place the dish in the top of the preheated oven. Bake for 15 minutes until the tomatoes are softened and the cheese topping is browned and bubbling.

2 tablespoons olive oil, plus extra for greasing

2 large tomatoes, firm but ripe

½ cup freshly grated Parmesan cheese

1 tablespoon chopped fresh parsley

Black pepper to taste

Serves 4

LETTUCE HEARTS WITH ANCHOVY DRESSING

2 romaine hearts

½ cup olive oil

1½ tablespoons white wine vinegar

1½ tablespoons mayonnaise

12 anchovy fillets

Freshly ground black pepper to taste

2 tablespoons chopped fresh parsley

4 cloves garlic, peeled and chopped and fried in olive oil (optional)

Serves 4

The fresh and clean taste of crispy lettuce hearts contrasts wonderfully with the potency of anchovies in this light salad (see right). The ingredients can be beautifully presented to make an eye-catching side dish for special occasions.

1   Wash and trim the lettuce hearts and set aside. To prepare the dressing, place the oil, vinegar, mayonnaise, four of the anchovy fillets and some freshly ground black pepper in a food processor. Blend the ingredients, then add the chopped fresh parsley. If you do not have a food processor, chop the anchovies finely and place them, along with the other ingredients, in a jar that has a lid. Shake the jar vigorously until all the ingredients are thoroughly combined.

2   To serve, cut the lettuce hearts into quarters and place two quarters on each plate. Drizzle the dressing over the lettuce hearts. Add a sprinkling of chopped and sautéed garlic if desired—this gives the dish a wonderful richness. Drape one anchovy fillet attractively over each lettuce heart quarter to decorate.

CARROTS WITH RAISINS & PINE NUTS

1 pound carrots

4 tablespoons mayonnaise

3 tablespoons olive oil

Juice of 1 lemon

⅓ cup seedless raisins

¼ cup pine nuts

Salt and pepper to taste

Snipped fresh chives to garnish

Serves 4–6

This sweet and creamy salad combines crunchy carrots and nuts with soft raisins and smooth mayonnaise.

1   Peel the carrots or scrape them clean, then grate them using the coarse blade on your grater. Place the grated carrot in a large mixing bowl and add the mayonnaise, olive oil and lemon juice. Mix well until all the ingredients are thoroughly blended.

2   Add the raisins and pine nuts and mix well, ensuring that all of the mixture is well combined with the dressing. Season with salt and pepper and sprinkle with snipped fresh chives to serve.

CARROTS WITH APPLE AND DATES

The honey, mint and dates in this salad give it a hint of the Middle East. Mix 1 tablespoon of lemon juice, 1 teaspoon of honey, ¼ teaspoon of fresh mint and a pinch of salt in a large bowl until well combined. Peel or scrape the carrots clean and add to the bowl with 2 peeled, cored and shredded Granny Smith apples, ¼ cup of pitted and chopped dates and 2 tablespoons of chopped fresh parsley. Toss well to mix, then serve.

Mayonnaise

1 egg yolk

½ teaspoon salt

1 teaspoon gluten-free Dijon mustard

1 cup oil (light olive or vegetable oil)

Juice of 1 small lemon

Makes 1 cup

Make sure that all the ingredients are at room temperature before making the mayonnaise. Combine the egg yolk, salt and mustard in a bowl and whisk the mixture thoroughly. Add the oil—to begin with, add a drop at a time, then slowly increase the flow, whisking the mixture continuously until all the oil is fully incorporated. (Avoid using virgin olive oil—this has too strong a flavor for mayonnaise.) Add the lemon juice and more salt if necessary. If the mixture is too thick, add a little warm water, mixing well. Mayonnaise can be made easily if using a food processor—place 1 egg yolk and 1 whole egg in the processor with the salt, mustard, lemon juice and half of the oil. Blend together and, with the machine still running, add the remaining oil in a steady stream. Adjust the seasoning to taste.

GREEN MAYONNAISE

Add watercress to the basic mayonnaise and process in a blender to break down the watercress thoroughly. Green mayonnaise is delicious on cold fish or with hard-boiled eggs.

GARLIC MAYONNAISE

Add 1 crushed clove of garlic—or more, to taste—to the basic mayonnaise. Mix thoroughly to combine the garlic evenly with the other ingredients. Garlic mayonnaise is excellent on fish or as a dip for large shrimp.

ITALIAN-STYLE "TONNATO" MAYONNAISE

Pound 2 anchovy fillets with 2 ounces (about ¼ cup, drained) of tuna fish in a little of the fish oil, adding a few finely chopped capers if desired, for additional flavor. Blend this mixture gradually into the basic mayonnaise. Italian-style "Tonnato" is particularly suitable for cold meats.

Pesto

2 cloves garlic, peeled

¼ cup pine nuts

Salt to taste

Shredded fresh basil (large bunch)

⅔ cup light olive oil

½ cup freshly grated Parmesan cheese

Makes about 1 cup

Pound the garlic, pine nuts and salt in a mortar using a pestle. Add the shredded basil leaves, a few at a time, and continue pounding until all the ingredients are fully ground down. Pour in the oil gradually and continue mixing. Finally, stir in the freshly grated Parmesan cheese. Alternatively, the ingredients may be blended together in a food processor. Pesto may be kept for a few days if necessary—seal it well and store in the refrigerator.

TOMATO PESTO

Pound 2 cloves of garlic with salt (to taste) and 10 sun-dried tomatoes in a mortar with a pestle. Add the shredded basil leaves, the olive oil and 1–2 chopped chilies to taste.

WHITE SAUCE

Make a paste by mixing a little of the milk into the cornstarch in a pan. Stir in the remaining cold milk, ensuring there are no lumps, place the pan over medium heat and slowly bring to a boil, stirring. Reduce the heat to simmer for 2–3 minutes until the sauce is thickened. Add salt and pepper.

1⅓ cups milk

2½ tablespoons cornstarch

Salt and pepper to taste

Makes 1⅓ cups sauce

CHEESE SAUCE

Add 1 cup of grated cheese and 1 tablespoon of gluten-free Dijon mustard to the basic white sauce, stirring over low heat until the cheese melts. Cheese sauce is good on many vegetable or chicken dishes.

PARSLEY SAUCE

Mix a handful of chopped fresh parsley into the white sauce directly before serving. This sauce is ideal with plain white fish such as cod.

LEMON SAUCE

Use a little less milk in the white sauce recipe and add the juice of 1 lemon as the mixture begins to thicken. This sauce is good on fish or vegetables.

CAPER SAUCE

Add 3 tablespoons of finely chopped capers to the prepared white sauce just before serving. Caper sauce is delicious with plain poached fish or chicken.

ONION SAUCE

Fry a chopped onion in a little butter until transparent, then mix this into the white sauce. Onion sauce is particularly good on vegetables such as cauliflower or zucchini.

VINAIGRETTE

Place all the ingredients in a jar which has a lid and shake vigorously. Alternatively, blend the ingredients together in a food processor. Use as required.

¼ cup white wine vinegar

1 cup olive oil

1 tablespoon gluten-free Dijon mustard

Pinch of salt

Makes 1¼ cups

VINAIGRETTE VARIATIONS

Any type of vinegar can be used: balsamic vinegar gives a deliciously sweet taste; sherry vinegar is stronger; scented vinegars add an exotic touch.

Any oil, or combination of oils, can be used: sesame oil gives a distinctive toasted flavor—only a little is recommended; extra virgin olive oil creates a strong, biting flavor; vegetable oil gives a lighter taste.

Add a tablespoon of chopped fresh herbs to the basic vinaigrette for a delightful aromatic touch, or a tablespoon of mayonnaise to create a creamy dressing. Chopped hard-boiled eggs are delicious mixed into the vinaigrette, as is raw sugar. A little chili powder can also be added for piquancy.

5 Desserts

RICE PUDDING BRÛLÉE

1 cup short-grain rice

1 cup water

1 stick cinnamon

Rind of 1 lemon, peeled using a potato peeler

½ cup sugar

Pinch of salt

1 quart (4 cups) whole milk

2 tablespoons superfine sugar

Serves 8

The contrast of the creamy rice and the sweet, crunchy caramel topping makes this traditional dessert a special treat

1   Place the rice and water in a large saucepan and bring to a boil. Cover and simmer for 8 minutes until the water is absorbed.

2   Add the cinnamon stick, the lemon rind, the sugar, salt and milk. Bring back to a boil, then reduce the heat to a very low setting and simmer gently for 30 minutes, stirring occasionally, until the rice is very tender and creamy.

3   Remove the cinnamon stick and lemon rind. While still hot, pour the rice and milk mixture into a 6 cup flameproof dish (a soufflé dish is ideal) or into 8 individual ramekins (approximately 3½-inches in diameter) and allow to cool. The rice should fill the containers completely.

4   Once the rice pudding is cold, sprinkle the superfine sugar over the top and place under a preheated broiler. Avoid sprinkling the sugar on to the edges of the dish, as the sugar will burn on to the dish and look untidy. Broil until the sugar starts to bubble and turn golden, but do not allow to burn. Once the top of the pudding is caramelized, remove from the heat very carefully (the dish or ramekins will be very hot) and allow to cool. Serve as soon as the pudding has cooled—it should not be kept for more than an hour or so as the caramel topping will begin to soften and dissolve, losing its crunchy texture.

FRUIT SALAD BRÛLÉE

1 pound mixed fresh fruit

⅔ cup heavy cream

¼ cup superfine sugar

Serves 6

The wonderful thing about this dessert is that you can prepare it with all of your favorite fruits, whether they be the classic, dependable favorites such as apples, pears, berries and bananas, or more exotic delicacies such as mango and kiwi fruit.

1   Chop the fruit into small pieces and spoon equal portions into 6 individual 3½-inch ramekins, filling them almost to the top.

2   Whip the cream until fairly stiff and, using a spatula, cover the individual fruit salads with the cream. Smooth out the tops so that the cream is level with the rims of the ramekins, then sprinkle liberally with sugar.

3   Place under a preheated broiler. Make sure that the heat is as high as it can be, and that you place the ramekins as close to the heat source as possible, so that the sugar caramelizes quickly, before the cream beneath it melts. Once caramelized, remove from the heat and allow to cool slightly before serving.

APRICOT SOUFFLÉ

Apricots lend a delicate flavor to this classic dessert. The ingredients required for soufflé are general kitchen fare—add a packet of dried apricots to your standard store cupboard contents so that you can always create a last-minute impressive finale to a meal.

1   Preheat the oven to 400°F, 200°C, gas mark 6. Grease either a 1 quart (4 cup) soufflé dish or 6 individual ramekins (approximately 3½-inches in diameter) with some melted butter. Dust with icing sugar and set aside.

2   Place the dried apricots in a saucepan and add enough water to just cover them. Bring to a boil and simmer uncovered for 20 minutes, until the fruit is very tender. Drain and allow to cool.

3   Place the apricots in a food processor and purée them. If you do not have a food processor, pass them through a sieve. Blend in the egg yolks and transfer the mixture to a bowl.

4   Whisk the egg whites until stiff, then carefully fold into the apricot mixture. Pour into the prepared soufflé dish and bake in the preheated oven for 20–25 minutes, or for 15 minutes if preparing individual portions. Remove from the oven, dust with confectioners' sugar and serve immediately, with light or heavy cream, if desired.

Butter for greasing

Confectioners' sugar for dusting

1½ cups dried apricots

4 large eggs, separated

Serves 4–6

HOT FRUIT SALAD

There is no reason why a fruit salad cannot be heated—in fact, a hot fruit salad makes a very satisfying and enjoyable dish on a cold winter's day. Any of your favorite fruits can be used—try those that are seasonably available.

1   Preheat the oven to 400°F, 200°C, gas mark 6. Grease a shallow ovenproof dish with melted butter.

2   Peel, core and slice the apples. Peel and divide the oranges, removing the pips and any excess pith. Cut the segments in half if too large. Peel and slice the bananas and kiwi fruit.

3   Place the fruit in layers into the prepared dish. Squeeze a little lemon juice over the fruit. Add the golden raisins or raisins and dot all over with the butter. Finally, pour over the rum (if using) and sprinkle with the dark brown sugar.

4   Place in the preheated oven for 30 minutes until the fruit is soft but still holds its shape. Serve hot with a scoop of rum and raisin or Vanilla Ice Cream (see page 106), or with English Custard Sauce (see page 108).

2 apples

2 oranges

2 bananas

2 kiwi fruit

Juice of 1 lemon

A few golden raisins or raisins

½ stick (4 tablespoons) unsalted butter, plus extra for greasing

3 tablespoons rum (optional)

3 tablespoons gluten-free dark brown sugar

Serves 6

PEARS BAKED IN CUSTARD

This recipe is similar to the classic French "clafoutis" which is usually made with cherries cooked in a light batter. The special ingredient that makes this particular dessert is the almond extract, which infuses the creamy custard with a nutty flavor to complement the sweet and succulent wedges of pear.

1 Preheat the oven to 350°F, 180°C, gas mark 4. Grease a 2½ x 12-inch ovenproof dish with melted butter.

2 Peel, core and slice the pears into 8 wedges each. If they are not ripe, poach them gently in a little water with sugar for about 5 minutes to soften them, so that they are just firm, then drain well. Spread the pears over the base of the buttered dish.

3 Beat the eggs with the sugar, almond extract and cornstarch. Stir in the cream and mix well.

4 Pour the custard over the pears and sprinkle the slivered almonds over the top. Place in the oven and cook for approximately 45 minutes until the custard has set. Serve warm with a sprinkling of confectioners' sugar.

Butter for greasing

5–6 ripe pears (according to size)

¼ cup superfine sugar

4 large eggs

1 teaspoon almond extract

1 teaspoon cornstarch

1⅓ cups heavy cream

1 tablespoon slivered almonds

Confectioners' sugar to serve

Serves 4–6

APPLES BAKED IN CUSTARD
Apples, such as Golden Delicious, can be substituted for the pears in the recipe above. Soften them in butter for about 5 minutes before placing them in the gratin dish with the custard. Mix in 1 tablespoon of Calvados instead of the almond extract, if preferred.

FIGS IN HONEY & WINE

Make this luxurious, yet simple, dessert (see left) during the summer, when figs are plentiful and at their best.

1 Wash the figs and place them in a large saucepan. Pour in enough white wine to cover the fruit, then add the honey.

2 Slowly bring to a boil, then simmer uncovered for approximately 15–20 minutes until the figs are just tender when pierced with a sharp knife. Be careful not to overcook the figs or they will disintegrate.

3 Turn off the heat, leave the figs in the pan and allow to cool and absorb the wine and honey syrup.

4 When cool, place two figs on each plate and serve with a scoop of Vanilla Ice Cream (see page 106) or some English Custard Sauce (see page 108).

8 fresh figs

White wine, approximately ½ bottle

½ cup honey

Serves 4

HONEY-POACHED ORANGES

6 small eating oranges

6 tablespoons honey

¼ cup sugar

Juice of 1 lemon

6 whole cloves

1 quart (4 cups) water

Serves 6

Cloves and oranges are a natural combination and here they are poached—and then served—in a delicious honey syrup. The warming cloves and honey contrast with the tang of the oranges.

1 Peel the oranges and remove all the pith. Place the honey, sugar, lemon juice, cloves and water in a saucepan and add the whole oranges.

2 Cook over high heat to boiling point. Then reduce the heat and simmer uncovered for 5–10 minutes, stirring occasionally.

3 Remove the oranges with a slotted spoon and place in a serving bowl. Boil the poaching liquid for 10 minutes to reduce it. Pour the hot syrup over the oranges and cool slightly. Cover and refrigerate for at least 3 hours until chilled before serving.

ORANGE & DATE SALAD

5 large eating oranges

½ cup chopped dates

A little brown sugar (if the oranges are not sweet)

Serves 4–6

This healthy fruit dessert requires very little time to put together and can be prepared well in advance.

1 Peel the oranges and remove all the pith. Divide them into segments and place them in a bowl.

2 Add the chopped dates to the oranges and a little sugar if necessary and stir. Leave to stand for at least an hour before serving so that the dates soften and absorb the orange juice.

ORANGE CRÈME CARAMEL

FOR THE CARAMEL

10 tablespoons sugar

4 tablespoons orange juice

Crème caramel is a traditional family favorite. Here I have flavored it delicately with fresh orange juice (see right), to give it a boost of added fruitiness.

1 Preheat the oven to 325°F, 160°C, gas mark 3. Place the sugar and orange juice in a small saucepan and boil over high heat for about 10 minutes, stirring occasionally until the sugar has dissolved and the liquid is thick and golden in color. Ensure that the syrup does not boil over. Remove from the heat and divide between 6 individual ⅔-cup crème caramel molds or custard cups or pour into the base of one large 3-cup mold.

2 Place the milk (or, for a creamier custard, equal quantities of milk and cream) in a saucepan with the orange rind. Cook over low heat and bring to just below boiling point.

3 Beat the eggs and the sugar in a bowl or jug—a jug is best for pouring the custard into the molds later. While still beating, gradually add the hot milk to the egg mixture.

4 Pour the custard carefully on to the caramel in the molds and sit the molds in a roasting pan which is half full of hot (but not boiling) water. The water should be roughly at a level with the middle of the moulds. Place the roasting pan containing the filled molds in the preheated oven for approximately 1 hour if using a large mold, or for 45 minutes if using individual molds. To make sure the custard has set, insert a knife into it and if it comes out clean, the custard is ready.

5 Allow to cool. For best results, refrigerate for at least 24 hours before serving, giving the caramel at the bottom of the molds time to dissolve slightly, thereby producing more syrup. To serve, carefully loosen the custard from the mold with a knife and turn out. Serve on its own, with light cream or Orange Syrup (see page 115).

FOR THE CUSTARD

2 cups milk or 1 cup milk and 1 cup cream

Grated rind of 1 orange

4 extra large eggs

¼ cup sugar

Serves 6

VANILLA CHEESECAKE

Light and refreshing, cheesecake is a classic favorite that never fails to please (see left). This basic recipe is delicious alone, but for a special occasion, give it a raspberry topping for a really luxurious flavor.

1 Preheat the oven to 325°F, 160°C, gas mark 3. Using melted butter, grease an 8-inch spring-form cake pan.

2 To make the crust, place the cornflakes, sugar and melted butter in a food processor and process until fairly fine, or place in a plastic bag and crush with a rolling pin. Place in the bottom of the prepared pan and press down with a metal spoon to create an even layer.

3 To make the filling, first rub the cottage cheese (or ricotta) through a sieve into a bowl. Separate the eggs, putting the whites and yolks into different bowls.

4 Mix the sugar and cornstarch together and add to the egg yolks. Beat until light and creamy. Work in the cheese, blending it in well. Then add the vanilla extract and sour cream. Mix everything together thoroughly.

5 Whisk the egg whites until stiff, then carefully fold into the egg and cheese mixture.

6 Pour the cheesecake mixture over the crust in the cake pan and bake in the preheated oven for 1 hour, until the filling has set. Turn off the heat but leave the cheesecake in the oven until it cools. When cold, chill the cheesecake for 24 hours before serving or topping.

FOR THE CRUST

Butter for greasing

4 cups cornflakes

¼ cup superfine sugar

½ stick (4 tablespoons) unsalted butter, melted

FOR THE FILLING

4 cups cottage cheese (or ricotta cheese)

3 extra large eggs

½ cup superfine sugar

2½ tablespoons cornstarch

I teaspoon gluten-free vanilla extract

⅔ cup sour cream

Serves 6–8

RASPBERRY GLAZE TOPPING

Clean 1 pound of fresh raspberries. Set aside half of them to decorate the top of the cheesecake. Make a purée with the rest of the berries, either by blending in a food processor or passing through a sieve.

Place the purée in a saucepan and add ¼ cup of superfine sugar. Set over low heat and cook gently to draw out the juice. Meanwhile, mix 1 tablespoon of cornstarch with 3 tablespoons of water and add to the raspberries in the saucepan. Bring to a boil and stir until thickened. Cook for 1–2 minutes, then add a pat of unsalted butter and stir until melted. Strain the purée and leave to cool. Spoon the cooled glaze over the cheesecake, decorate with the whole raspberries and chill until ready to serve.

PINEAPPLE GLAZE TOPPING

Use pineapple as an alternative to a berry topping for cheesecake. Drain a 20-ounce can of crushed pineapple and use approximately 1 cup of fruit. Place this in a pan and add ¼ cup superfine sugar, 1 tablespoon of cornstarch and a pat of unsalted butter. Cook as for Raspberry Glaze Topping, above.

APPLE TART

FOR THE TART DOUGH

I cup cornmeal

½ stick (4 tablespoons) unsalted butter, chilled and cut into pieces

3 teaspoons superfine sugar

I large egg, beaten

FOR THE APPLE FILLING

4 large sweet apples (such as Golden Delicious)

½ stick (4 tablespoons) unsalted butter

¼ cup sugar

Juice of I lemon

⅔ cup apricot preserves

Serves 6

When making pastry, an excellent gluten-free alternative to conventional flour is cornmeal. This recipe for apple tart uses sweet apples for a softer, more delicate flavor. The pastry shell does not need to be baked blind (partially baked) before being filled. An apricot glaze will give the tart an attractive finish.

1   Preheat the oven to 350°F, 180°C, gas mark 4. Process the cornmeal, butter and sugar in a food processor. Alternatively, place the cornmeal and sugar in a mixing bowl and rub in the butter with your fingertips until the mixture has a crumbly texture, similar to that of breadcrumbs.

2   Once the cornmeal and butter are well blended, add the beaten egg and mix it in with a palate knife to make a dough. If the pastry is too dry and crumbly, add a drop or two of water to help it hold together. Make a ball with the pastry using your hands.

3   Place the ball of pastry between two lengths of plastic wrap and carefully flatten it with a rolling pin until you have a fairly even sheet of pastry that is large enough to line a 10-inch flan or tart pan. Use a pan that has a removable base.

4   Take off the top piece of plastic wrap and, using the bottom piece to help you, lift up the pastry and turn it over into the pan. There is no need to grease the pan first, as the pastry is oily enough itself. Remove the plastic wrap and press the pastry into the pan. Work the dough up the sides of the pan, cutting off any excess pastry and patching up where necessary. Try to handle the pastry as little as possible to stop it becoming sticky. Cool the pastry shell in the refrigerator while you proceed to the next step.

5   To make the filling, peel, quarter and core the apples and slice them fairly thinly and evenly. Melt the butter in a large skillet and place the sliced apples in it with the sugar and lemon juice. Cook gently for approximately 10 minutes, until the apples begin to soften. Turn the slices over from time to time and shake the pan to ensure that all the apples are evenly cooked. Try not to break them or brown them.

6   Remove the cooked apples from the pan and place them in the pastry shell. Arrange them attractively, in overlapping circles, for example. Set aside the buttery juices.

7   Place the tart on a baking sheet in the preheated oven for 25–30 minutes until the edges of the crust are golden brown. Take out of the oven, remove the outer rim of the tin and pour over the reserved buttery juices.

8   To make apricot glaze, place some apricot preserves in a small saucepan and cook over low heat until runny. Strain out the fruit. Pour the remaining syrup over the apple tart. Serve warm or cold with cream or ice cream.

LEMON CUSTARD TART

The clean, refreshing taste of this tart (see above) makes it ideal for serving after a heavy meal. This recipe works just as well using limes, in which case you will need three pieces of fruit.

1 Preheat the oven to 350°F, 180°C, gas mark 4. Prepare the tart dough pastry as for Apple Tart (see opposite) and mold it into a 10-inch flan or tart pan. Line the pan loosely with foil and fill with dried beans, uncooked rice or ceramic baking beans (alternatively, make a few incisions in the base using a sharp knife) and place in the oven to bake blind for 15 minutes. Remove from the oven, discard the foil and beans (if using) and leave to cool.

2 Place the eggs and sugar in a food processor and blend thoroughly. Or put in a bowl and beat with a hand-whisk until fairly creamy. Add the grated lemon rind and lemon juice to the egg and sugar mixture. Stir to combine all the ingredients, then add the heavy cream and mix well.

3 Pour this mixture into the partly-baked pastry shell, then place it on a baking sheet and return to the oven for another 25–30 minutes until the custard has set. Remove from the oven and allow to cool completely, then remove the outer rim of the pan and place on a plate. Sprinkle with confectioners' sugar and serve either alone or with whipped cream. For an attractive presentation, cut paper strips of the same size and place them on the tart, overlapping them to make a pattern of your choice, such as the diamond pattern shown above. Dust with confectioners' sugar, then remove the paper strips carefully to reveal the pattern.

10-inch tart shell as for Apple Tart (see opposite)

4 large eggs

10 tablespoons superfine sugar

Grated rind and juice of 2 lemons

¾ cup and 1 tablespoon heavy cream

Confectioners' sugar for dusting

Serves 6

ALMOND MERINGUE GÂTEAU

Corn oil for greasing

4 egg whites

1 cup and 2 tablespoons superfine sugar

1 teaspoon cornstarch

2 teaspoons gluten-free vanilla extract

½ teaspoon white wine vinegar

1 cup ground almonds

1 cup heavy cream

Confectioners' sugar for dusting

8 whole unblanched almonds

Raspberry or Strawberry Coulis to serve
(see page 109)

Serves 6

This simple but divine meringue gâteau (see below) can also be made using ground hazelnuts. Serve it with a raspberry or strawberry coulis.

1   Preheat the oven to 375°F, 190°C, gas mark 5. Grease two 8-inch layer cake pans with corn oil and line the bottoms with parchment paper.

2   Make a meringue with the egg whites and sugar (see opposite page). Quickly whisk the cornstarch, vanilla extract and vinegar into the meringue, then gently fold in the ground nuts. Divide evenly and spoon into the prepared pans. Bake in the center of the oven for 35 minutes.

3   Remove from the oven and allow the meringues to cool in the tins. Once cool, carefully turn them out, running a palette knife around the edge of the meringues to loosen them from the pan. Remove the lining.

4   Whisk the cream until thick, not buttery. Place one of the meringues on a cake stand and spread the whipped cream evenly over the top. Place the other meringue on top. Sift confectioners' sugar over the gâteau, decorate with almonds and serve with a Fruit Coulis (see page 109).

MAKING MERINGUE

Place 4 egg whites in a large, clean mixing bowl and whisk until stiff. Then whisk in 1 cup and 2 tablespoons superfine sugar, adding 1 tablespoon of sugar at a time. Whisk the mixture well between each addition.

MAKING MERINGUE NESTS

To make meringue nests, preheat the oven to 225°F, 100°C, gas mark ¼. Fill a large pastry bag (fitted with a medium-sized star tip) with meringue mixture (see above). Line two baking sheets with parchment. Draw eight 5½-inch circles on the paper with a pencil, turn the paper over and pipe a continuous spiral of meringue to fill each circle, starting in the center. Pipe a second layer on the edge of each circle to form a wall. Bake for 4–5 hours. Turn off the oven but leave the nests inside until cold. Store in an airtight container for up to 3 weeks. Fill the nests with whipped cream and fruit or Vanilla Ice Cream (see page 106) drizzled with a Fruit Coulis (see page 109) or Chocolate Sauce (see page 109).

ROLLED COCONUT MERINGUE

This spectacular dessert is easier to make than it appears. Although any creamy filling can be used, a mixture of tangy home-made lemon curd and cream contrasts well with the sweet meringue. Alternatively, the cream can be flavored with melted chocolate, coffee liqueur or Strawberry Coulis (see page 109).

4 egg whites

1 cup and 2 tablespoons superfine sugar

3 tablespoons cornstarch

2 teaspoons gluten-free vanilla extract

1 teaspoon white wine vinegar

1⅓ cups shredded, sweetened coconut

¼ cup heavy cream

½ cup home-made Lemon Curd (see page 108)

Confectioners' sugar for dusting

Serves 6–8

1   Preheat the oven to 275°F, 140°C, gas mark 1. Line a 12 x 7-inch jelly roll pan with parchment paper.

2   Prepare the meringues using the egg whites and sugar (see above). Quickly whisk in the cornstarch, vanilla extract and vinegar, then carefully fold in the shredded coconut.

3   Spread the meringue evenly over the prepared pan and bake in the center of the oven for 40 minutes. Remove from the oven, cover with a clean, damp dish towel and leave to cool in the pan.

4   Pour the cream into a chilled bowl and whisk until thick (but not buttery), then fold in the lemon curd.

5   Cut a sheet of parchment paper slightly larger than the pan used to bake the meringue. Lay it on a work surface, then turn the cooled meringue out on to the paper. Peel off the paper that originally lined the pan. Spread the lemon cream evenly over the meringue and roll it up from one of the short ends, using the parchment paper beneath it to help you push the roll along. Do not worry if it cracks a little, as it will be delicious anyhow.

6   Transfer the rolled meringue to a serving dish. Cover it loosely with foil and chill until ready to serve. Dust lightly with confectioners' sugar.

Vanilla Ice Cream

3 eggs, separated

¼ cup sugar

¾ cup and 1 tablespoon heavy cream

1 teaspoon gluten-free vanilla extract

Serves 6

Serve this simple vanilla ice cream with a rich chocolate or fruity sauce, or as an accompaniment to fruit tarts, crisps and pies.

1   Put the egg yolks and sugar in a bowl with 3 tablespoons of water and place over a saucepan of simmering water—this allows the mixture to be surrounded by a gentle heat, which will heat it through slowly, helping to prevent it curdling. Stir until the mixture begins to thicken to a consistency that will coat the back of a spoon. Remove the custard from the heat and continue stirring until cooled.

2   Beat the egg whites in a bowl until stiff. In a separate bowl, beat the double cream until thick, then stir in the vanilla extract.

3   Fold the cooled custard into the cream, then carefully fold in the egg whites. Pour this ice cream mixture into a 1 quart (4 cup) loaf tin or plastic box, cover and freeze.

4   When ready to serve, run a sharp knife around the container and turn the ice cream out of the mold on to a serving platter. Slice the ice cream and serve each slice with a generous helping of Chocolate Sauce (see page 109) or Raspberry Sauce (see below).

Chocolate Chip Ice Cream with Raspberry Sauce

FOR THE ICE CREAM

3 egg whites

⅔ cup superfine sugar

1 cup heavy cream

¼ pound bittersweet chocolate, grated

1 teaspoon gluten-free vanilla extract

FOR THE RASPBERRY SAUCE

½ pound raspberries, fresh or frozen

Superfine sugar to taste

3 tablespoons gluten-free cassis liqueur (optional)

Serves 6

The flecks of chocolate in this recipe work remarkably well with a luscious raspberry sauce.

1   Beat the egg whites in a bowl until stiff. Gradually add half the sugar, a little at a time, beating continuously until the mixture is stiff and glossy.

2   In a separate bowl, whip the cream until thick, gradually adding the rest of the sugar, the grated chocolate and the vanilla extract.

3   Fold the egg white mixture into the whipped cream and chocolate. Pour into a 1 quart (4 cup) loaf tin or plastic box, cover and freeze.

4   Meanwhile, place the raspberries in a food processor and blend into a purée, then sieve to remove the seeds. (If you do not have a food processor, just pass the raspberries through a sieve.) Add a little sugar to taste and stir in the cassis liqueur, if using.

5   Run a sharp knife around the edge of the container and turn out the ice cream. Cut into slices and serve drizzled generously with raspberry sauce.

STRAWBERRY SORBET

Besides being wonderfully refreshing, sorbet is very easily made, as it is simply iced sugared water which is given body with beaten egg whites and flavor with a fruit coulis or purée.

1 Rub the prepared strawberries through a very fine mesh sieve into a bowl to make a purée. Place the sugar and water in a saucepan and boil for 5 minutes to make a syrup. Allow to cool completely, then pour the syrup into the fruit purée and mix well. Place the mixture in a plastic box in the freezer for 1–2 hours until half frozen.

2 Remove the sorbet mixture from the freezer and beat until smooth. Fold in the stiffly beaten egg whites and return to the freezer for a further 1–2 hours until fairly hard. Serve directly from the freezer.

1 pound strawberries, washed and hulled

¼ cup sugar

⅔ cup water

2 egg whites, stiffly beaten

Serves 4–6

COFFEE PRALINE MOUSSE

Praline provides a crunchy topping to contrast with the smooth texture of this tempting coffee mousse.

1 Place the milk in a saucepan and heat over medium heat without bringing to a boil. When the milk is steaming, stir in the coffee. Beat the egg yolks and sugar in a mixing bowl until thick and creamy, then gradually add the flavored milk. Return to the pan and stir continuously over low heat until the custard thickens—it should coat the back of a wooden spoon. Do not allow the mixture to boil or it will curdle. Leave to cool.

2 Dissolve the gelatin in 4 tablespoons of hot water in a small saucepan. Stir vigorously and allow to stand for 1–2 minutes. If not completely dissolved, place over very low heat for a few seconds and stir. Do not allow the liquid to boil. Once transparent and runny, stir a little of the custard mixture into the gelatin, then pour it back into the remaining custard. Stir well and allow to cool completely and begin to set—place it in the refrigerator to accelerate the process. Ensure it does not set completely.

3 Whip the cream a little and fold into the custard. In a separate bowl, whisk the egg whites until stiff. Then carefully fold these into the mixture. Pour the mousse into a 1 quart (4 cup) mold or soufflé dish and refrigerate for at least 2 hours. To serve, sprinkle liberally with the praline.

2 cups milk

3 tablespoons strong coffee

3 large eggs, separated

6 tablespoons superfine sugar

3½ teaspoons (about 1½ envelopes) unflavored gelatin

7 tablespoons heavy cream

Serves 6

MAKING PRALINE

Place ½ cup of granulated sugar and 1½ tablespoons of water in a saucepan and heat gently until dissolved. Boil until golden then stir in 1 cup of toasted slivered almonds. Turn the mixture out on to an oiled baking sheet to cool, then crush with a pestle in a mortar or blend in a food processor until crumbly.

Lemon Curd

1 cup and 2 tablespoons sugar

Grated rind and juice of 2 lemons

⅓ cup unsalted butter, cut into pieces

3 eggs

Makes approximately 1 pound

There are many uses for this tart, creamy lemon sauce—for instance, as a topping for baked desserts or, for a simple pudding, as a filling for a pastry case, along with some fresh whipped cream.

1 Place the sugar in a bowl over a small saucepan of simmering water and add the lemon juice and rind. Stir the mixture occasionally as it slowly heats until the sugar has dissolved completely. Stir in the pieces of butter until they have melted and are fully blended with the sugar and lemon. Remove from the heat and leave to cool.

2 Beat the eggs in a separate bowl and pour the cooled lemon and sugar mixture on to them. Strain and place over the pan of simmering water. Cook over this gentle heat and stir until the lemon curd is thick enough to coat the back of a wooden spoon.

3 Remove from the heat and pour the lemon curd into warmed, sterilized, clean jars. Leave to cool and thicken for 24 hours. Lemon curd will keep for 1–2 weeks if refrigerated in an airtight container.

English Custard Sauce

2 cups milk, plus 3 tablespoons extra for mixing with the cornstarch

2 teaspoons cornstarch

2 tablespoons superfine sugar

2 eggs

1 teaspoon gluten-free vanilla extract

Makes 2½ cups

This rich custard sauce is warming and filling and delicious served with stewed fruits, pies and crumbles.

1 Pour the milk into a saucepan and heat over low heat until the milk is hot, but not boiling.

2 Blend the cornstarch with the remaining cold milk, then stir into the hot milk. (The cornstarch stabilizes the custard, making it less likely to curdle.) Slowly bring to a boil and cook for a few seconds. Remove the pan from the heat and stir in the sugar. Leave to cool, stirring occasionally.

3 Beat the eggs in a bowl. Stir in some of the milk and cornstarch mixture, then pour back into the saucepan with the remaining milk. Heat gently, stirring constantly, until the custard reaches the right consistency to coat the back of a wooden spoon. Do not boil the mixture.

4 Remove from the heat, stir in the vanilla extract and allow to cool a little, stirring continuously to prevent a skin from forming on the top.

5 Use immediately. English Custard Sauce makes an ideal accompaniment to Apple Tart (see page 102) or Hot Fruit Salad (see page 95).

FRUIT COULIS

A coulis is a puréed sauce which is either savory or sweet (above, left and front are a strawberry and a raspberry coulis). The consistency should be pourable. For a fresh fruit coulis, process the cleaned fruit in a blender and strain out the pips or fibers if necessary (as with raspberries, for instance). Add sugar, lemon juice and liqueur for extra flavor, if desired.

DRIED APRICOT PUREE

To make apricot purée (above, right), soak 1¾ cups of dried apricots in water for a few hours, then drain and cook in 2 cups of water for 20 minutes until soft. Allow to cool a little, then purée with the cooking liquid, adding a little more water if necessary. Sugar should not be needed.

CHOCOLATE SAUCE

Chop ½ pound of bittersweet chocolate. Then place in a bowl and place over a saucepan of simmering water, ensuring the bowl does not touch the water in the pan. Heat gently until the chocolate has melted. Add heavy cream to make the sauce richer. For extra flavor, add orange juice or a liqueur.

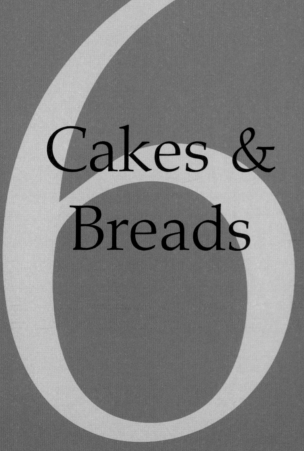

6 Cakes & Breads

CHOCOLATE HAZELNUT CAKE

This decadent, rich and moist pudding-like cake (see left) will keep well for several days if stored in an airtight container. It can be made using ground almonds in place of the hazelnuts.

1   To prepare the cake, preheat the oven to 350°F, 180°C, gas mark 4. Butter a 10-inch spring-form cake pan and line the base with parchment paper.

2   Place the chocolate into a medium-sized mixing bowl and stand this over a saucepan of gently simmering water. Stir until the chocolate has melted. Add the butter, stir until evenly blended with the chocolate, then remove from the heat.

3   Put the egg yolks and sugar in a large mixing bowl and whisk until thick and creamy. Stir in the yogurt and hazelnuts, then add the melted chocolate and butter and mix well.

4   Whisk the egg whites until stiff. Fold a quarter into the chocolate mixture to loosen it a little, then gently fold in the rest.

5   Pour the mixture into the prepared pan and bake in the center of the oven for 60–70 minutes until the cake is well risen and feels firm to the touch. Use the skewer test (see opposite) to ensure the cake is cooked through. Leave to cool in the pan.

6   When the cake is cold, run a palette knife around the side to loosen it from the edges of the pan. Remove the cake from the pan, carefully transfer it on to a serving plate and peel off the lining paper.

7   To prepare the chocolate icing, melt the chocolate in a small bowl placed over a saucepan of simmering water and stir in the butter.

8   Spread the chocolate icing over the top of the cake with a palette knife and mark it into swirls. Once the icing has set, cut the cake into slices and serve with heavy cream poured over it.

FOR THE CAKE

10 ounces good quality bittersweet chocolate, coarsely chopped

1½ sticks (12 tablespoons) unsalted butter, cut into small cubes, plus extra for greasing

6 large eggs, separated

½ cup, packed dark brown sugar

½ cup plain yogurt

2½ scant cups ground hazelnuts

Heavy cream to serve (optional)

FOR THE CHOCOLATE ICING

4 ounces good quality bittersweet chocolate, coarsely chopped

2 tablespoons unsalted butter, cut into small cubes, plus extra for greasing

Serves 6–8

BUTTER CREAM ICING

For a less chocolatey topping, beat ½ stick (4 tablespoons) of butter with a wooden spoon until light and fluffy. Gradually sift in ¼ cup of confectioners' sugar until the desired texture and level of sweetness are achieved. Spread the butter cream icing over the cake and decorate with grated chocolate. This recipe produces enough icing to cover an 8-inch cake.

Chocolate Hazelnut Cake is delicious with orange or coffee icing, both of which can be made by flavoring the basic butter cream icing recipe given here. For orange icing, blend 1 teaspoon of finely grated orange rind with 1 tablespoon of orange juice and mix into the icing. For coffee flavor, dissolve 1 teaspoon of instant coffee in 1 tablespoon of hot water and mix into the icing.

CHOCOLATE ROULADE

For the best results, the chocolate sponge for this roulade should be made the day before, but it can be used sooner, so long as it is left to stand for at least two hours after baking.

1   Preheat the oven to 375°F, 190°C, gas mark 5. Line a 15½ x 10½-inch jelly roll pan with parchment paper, allowing the paper to sit a little above the sides of the tin. Cut a second sheet of parchment to the same size and set aside.

2   Place the pieces of chocolate in a bowl sitting over a saucepan of gently simmering water. Stir until the chocolate melts. Mix in ¼ cup of hot water—if the chocolate becomes lumpy, continue stirring until smooth.

3   Place the egg yolks in a large mixing bowl and whisk with the sugar until light and fluffy. Gradually whisk in the melted chocolate.

4   Beat the egg whites until soft peaks form. Fold a quarter of this into the chocolate mixture to loosen it a little, then carefully fold in the remainder. Pour the mixture into the prepared pan and spread it evenly into all four corners. Bake in the center of the preheated oven for 20 minutes or until well risen and firm to the touch.

5   Grease one side of the reserved sheet of parchment. Remove the cooked sponge from the oven and immediately cover the top with the parchment, oiled-side down. Cover with a clean, damp dish towel and leave to stand for a few hours or until the next day.

6   Uncover the jelly roll pan, remove the top sheet of parchment and set aside. Sift with confectioners' sugar, re-cover with the parchment and, holding the sponge firmly between parchment and pan, turn upside-down on to the work surface. Remove the pan and peel off the lining paper.

7   Pour the cream into a chilled bowl, add the vanilla extract and whisk until thick, but not buttery. Spread the whipped cream evenly over the sponge and roll it up, starting at a short end. Use the parchment beneath the sponge to help you push the roll along. Do not worry if the sponge cracks a little as you roll it – this is normal. Once rolled up, dust the roulade with confectioners' sugar – this helps to cover any imperfections on the surface.

8   Carefully lift the roulade on to a board. Loosely cover with foil and chill for 2 hours before serving with a freshly-made Raspberry or Strawberry Coulis (see page 109).

5 ounces good quality bittersweet chocolate, coarsely chopped

4 large eggs, separated

½ cup and 1 tablespoon superfine sugar

Butter for greasing

Confectioners' sugar for dusting

¾ cup and 1 tablespoon heavy cream

½ teaspoon gluten-free vanilla extract

Raspberry or Strawberry Coulis (see page 109) to serve (optional)

Serves 8

THE SKEWER TEST

To test if a cake is cooked through, pierce it to the center with a skewer. If the skewer comes out clean and dry, the cake is ready. If not, the cake should be cooked for a little longer.

CHOCOLATE WALNUT CAKE

The delightfully gooey texture of this cake is very much like that of brownies. The nuts provide richness and flavor.

Butter for greasing

2½ scant cups ground walnuts

½ cup unsweetened cocoa powder

5 large eggs

1¼ cups superfine sugar

Confectioners' sugar for dusting

Serves 6–8

1 Preheat the oven to 375°F, 190°C, gas mark 5. Grease and line the base of a 8-inch non-stick layer cake pan.

2 Mix the ground walnuts and cocoa powder with two of the eggs. Once you have a stiff paste, mix in the remaining three eggs, one at a time. Slowly work in the sugar, making sure that everything is well-mixed.

3 Spoon the cake mixture into the buttered and lined cake pan. Place the pan in the preheated oven and bake for approximately 60 minutes. Towards the end of the cooking time, use the skewer test (see page 113) to ensure the cake is cooked through. Cool a little, turn out and remove the lining paper. Place it, right side up, on a wire rack until ready to serve.

4 Dust with confectioners' sugar. Serve this cake alone as a tea-time snack, or with heavy cream or Vanilla Ice Cream (see page 106) as a dessert.

LEMON POLENTA & ALMOND CAKE

Polenta gives this lemon and almond cake an unusual and delightfully crunchy texture. The lemon juice and rind provide a hint of sharpness that complements the earthy flavor of the almonds.

1 cup (2 sticks) butter, slightly salted, plus extra for greasing

1 cup and 2 tablespoons superfine sugar

4 large eggs

2 scant cups ground almonds

1 teaspoon gluten-free vanilla extract

1 cup fine grain polenta (or cornmeal)

Grated rind and juice of 1 lemon

1 teaspoon gluten-free baking powder

Serves 6–8

1 Preheat the oven to 375°F, 190°C, gas mark 5. Use melted butter to grease a 8-inch non-stick cake pan. Line the base with a circle of wax paper, cut to size and greased with melted butter.

2 Beat the butter with the sugar in a mixing bowl until light and creamy. Then gradually beat in the eggs, one at a time.

3 Stir in the ground almonds and vanilla extract until they are thoroughly combined with the sugar, butter and egg mixture, then fold in the polenta, lemon rind and juice and the baking powder.

4 Spoon the cake mixture into the prepared cake pan and place in the preheated oven. Bake for 60–70 minutes. Use the skewer test (see page 113) to ensure the cake is cooked through—it should feel moist to the touch and be fairly brown on the top surface. Serve the cake, right side up, alone or with a generous spoonful of mascarpone cheese.

ALMOND SPONGE CAKE

This light, moist sponge cake (see above) is easy to make and its flavor is gloriously complemented by the tangy orange syrup.

1 Preheat the oven to 350°F, 180°C, gas mark 4. Use melted butter to grease a 8-inch non-stick cake pan. Cut a circle of wax paper to fit the base, place it in the pan and grease with butter.

2 Whisk the egg yolks with the sugar until light and creamy. Then slowly fold in the ground almonds and lemon rind. Beat the egg whites until stiff and stir a little of this into the yolk and sugar mixture to soften it, then gently fold in the rest.

3 Pour the cake mixture into the prepared cake pan and bake in the preheated oven for approximately 40 minutes. Use the skewer test (see page 113) to ensure the cake is cooked through.

4 When the cake is cooked, remove it from the oven and leave to cool. Pass a knife around the edge of the cake to loosen it from the sides of the pan, then turn out on to a plate and remove the lining paper. Turn the right way up and make a few deep holes in the top of the cake with a skewer.

5 To make the orange syrup, place the orange juice, sugar and cinnamon stick in a saucepan and simmer for 5–6 minutes, allowing the sugar to dissolve. Leave to cool, then pour over the cake—the syrup is absorbed through the holes. Top the cake with the cinnamon stick for decoration.

FOR THE CAKE

Butter for greasing

5 eggs, separated

¾ cup and 2 tablespoons superfine sugar

1¾ cups ground almonds

Grated rind of 1 lemon

FOR THE ORANGE SYRUP

Juice of 2 oranges

¼ cup sugar

1 stick cinnamon

Serves 6–8

ORANGE & ALMOND CAKE

Because it is made with fresh whole oranges, this soft, pudding-like cake (see left) has a wonderfully strong citrus flavor.

Butter for greasing
2 large oranges
6 large eggs, separated
1¼ cups superfine sugar
2¼ scant cups ground almonds
Serves 6–8

1 Preheat the oven to 350°F, 180°C, gas mark 4. Grease a 9-inch non-stick cake pan. Cut a circle of parchment to fit the base, grease it with melted butter and use to line the base.

2 Place the whole, unpeeled oranges into a saucepan of water and boil for 2 hours until completely soft. Alternatively, cook them in a pressure cooker for half an hour.

3 Remove from the pan and cool slightly. Then cut them open and remove the seeds. Place the oranges in a food processor and blend with the egg yolks. Alternatively, mash the oranges with a fork and whisk with the egg yolks in a mixing bowl.

4 Add the sugar and ground almonds to the orange and egg mixture, a little at a time, and continue blending until all the ingredients are well-combined. Transfer to a large bowl.

5 Beat the egg whites until stiff in a separate bowl. Now fold these carefully into the orange mixture.

6 Pour the cake mixture into the prepared pan and bake in the preheated oven for 60–70 minutes. Use the skewer test (see page 113) to ensure the cake is cooked through. When cooked, remove from the oven and allow to cool before turning out.

7 Run a knife around the edge of the cake to loosen it from the sides of the pan, turn out on to a plate and remove the lining paper. Then turn the cake the right way up. The cake may be iced with orange flavored Butter Cream Icing (see page 112) or Marmalade Sauce (see below), or served with crème fraîche, mascarpone cheese or fresh strawberries.

MARMALADE SAUCE

This is the ideal topping for Orange and Almond cake. To make it, mix ½ cup of fine-cut orange marmalade with ¾ cup of orange juice (which is the juice of roughly 2 oranges) in a saucepan. Place the pan over medium heat and bring the liquid to a boil, stirring constantly to ensure the marmalade dissolves and mixes with the orange juice. Remove the pan from the heat. Mix 3 tablespoons of arrowroot with 3 tablespoons of water in a cup and stir this into the hot orange liquid. Reheat gently, stirring constantly until the sauce thickens. If preferred, the orange peel can be removed using a sieve. Consume the sauce either hot or cold. This recipe makes approximately 1⅓ cups of sauce.

For a rich and creamy sauce, strain out the peel, allow to cool, then mix in 3 tablespoons of heavy cream.

DATE & BROWN SUGAR MUFFINS

½ stick (4 tablespoons) unsalted butter (or margarine), plus extra for greasing

¼ cup soft dark brown sugar, plus extra for sprinkling

2 large eggs

¾ cup and 1 tablespoon buttermilk

⅔ cup cornmeal

1 cup brown rice flour

1 rounded teaspoon gluten-free baking powder

¼ cup chopped dates

Makes 6 large (or 12 small) muffins

These tempting muffins (see right) are ideal served with afternoon tea, but are just as good for a sweet and fruity breakfast.

1 Preheat the oven to 400°F, 200°C, gas mark 6. Use a little butter to grease a 6-hole muffin pan. (If you prefer smaller muffins, use a 12-hole muffin.)

2 Using a wooden spoon, beat together the butter (or margarine) and sugar until light and creamy. Beat in the eggs one at a time, then, once they are thoroughly blended with the butter and sugar, stir in the buttermilk. (Ordinary milk, soured with a squeeze of lemon juice, may be used in place of the buttermilk.)

3 Mix the cornmeal, rice flour and baking powder in a separate bowl, then gradually fold this into the butter, eggs and buttermilk mixture. Finally, add the chopped dates.

4 Divide the mixture into 6 (or 12) portions and spoon these evenly into the greased muffin pan. Sprinkle the tops of each portion with a little brown sugar.

5 Place the muffin pan on a baking sheet and put in the top half of the preheated oven. Bake the muffins for 25–30 minutes (or for 20 minutes if making smaller muffins). Test the muffins using the skewer test (see page 113) to determine whether or not they are cooked through. Remove them from the oven when thoroughly cooked and allow to cool in the pan. Turn out on to a wire rack and serve fresh—just cooled—cut in half and spread with butter.

BANANA MUFFINS
Add 1 very ripe mashed banana to the basic batter in place of the dates to make tasty and fragrant banana muffins.

RAISIN OR APRICOT MUFFINS
Use ⅓ cup of seedless raisins in place of the dates for fruity raisin muffins. Other ready-to-eat dried fruits, such as apricots, can also be used. These should be chopped very finely.

SAVORY CHEESE MUFFINS
The basic muffin recipe given above can be used to make delicious savory muffins. Follow the steps above but omit the sugar and dates. Instead, beat the butter with ½ cup of grated Parmesan cheese and season the mixture with plenty of freshly ground black pepper. Do not add salt, as the cheese is salty enough. Add this mixture to the basic muffin batter, then sprinkle the tops of the muffins with a little more grated Parmesan cheese before baking them as for the sweet muffins, above.

FRUIT & NUT LOAF

Butter for greasing

1¾ sticks (14 tablespoons) unsalted butter or shortening

1 cup sugar

4 large eggs

1⅓ cups cornmeal

1 teaspoon gluten-free baking powder

1 teaspoon cinnamon

½ scant cup chopped nuts (any type)

⅓ cup seeded raisins

Serves 6–8

Cornmeal is readily available in supermarkets and can be used to make delicious teacakes, such as this fruit and nut loaf (see below), which keeps well for several days.

1   Preheat the oven to 350°F, 180°C, gas mark 4. Using butter and parchment paper, grease and line a 9 x 5-inch non-stick loaf pan.

2   Beat the margarine with a wooden spoon in a bowl until light and creamy. Add the sugar and continue beating, then beat in the eggs, one at a time.

3   Work in the cornmeal, baking powder and cinnamon. Once all of the ingredients are combined, add the nuts and raisins.

4   Spoon the mixture into the greased and lined loaf pan and gently even out the batter. Place in the preheated oven and bake for 60 minutes. Use the skewer test (see page 113) to ensure the cake is thoroughly cooked.

5   Allow to cool, then run a knife around the edge of the loaf to loosen it from the pan. Turn out and cut into slices to serve, alone or with butter.

SAND CAKE

This cake has a dry, compact texture which may be complemented by a fruit compote or creamy fruit dessert. Alternatively, serve it alone as a teacake. The taste of sandcake improves with standing—after making it, wait for a day to allow the flavors to mature.

1   Preheat the oven to 350°F, 180°C, gas mark 4. Grease an 8-inch non-stick layer cake pan or square cake pan with melted butter.

2   Beat the butter and sugar together with a wooden spoon in a mixing bowl until light and creamy. Add the egg yolks one at a time, until all the ingredients are thoroughly blended. Mix in the ground almonds, the lemon rind and juice and finally, the cornstarch.

3   Beat the egg whites until stiff and forming soft peaks. Add a little of this to the cake mixture to soften it. Carefully fold in the remaining egg whites with a large metal spoon.

4   Spoon the mixture into the prepared pan and bake in the preheated oven for 50–60 minutes. Test that the cake is cooked using the skewer test (see page 113).

5   When cooked, remove from the oven and allow to cool slightly. Then turn out on to a wire rack and serve.

1¾ sticks (14 tablespoons) unsalted butter, plus extra for greasing

¾ cup and 2 tablespoons superfine sugar

3 eggs, separated

½ scant cup ground almonds

Grated rind and juice of ½ lemon

1½ cups cornstarch (measure by dip and sweep method)

Serves 6–8

RICE CAKE

Rice cake has a wonderful creamy flavor and soft texture. Serve slices or wedges with a Fruit Coulis (see page 109).

1   Place the rice in the milk with a pinch of salt. Heat to simmer and cook for approximately 30 minutes, until the rice is soft and has absorbed all of the milk. Stir and allow to cool a little.

2   Preheat the oven to 350°F, 180°C, gas mark 4. Grease an 8-inch spring-form cake pan with butter and line the base with parchment paper.

3   Beat the butter and sugar together until light and creamy. Add the egg yolks one at a time, then stir in the cooked rice and mix well until fully blended. Whisk the egg whites until stiff, then fold them into the mixture.

4   Pour the mixture into the greased cake pan and bake in the preheated oven for 45–50 minutes until cooked through. Test that the cake is cooked using the skewer test (see page 113). Once cooked, remove from the oven and allow to cool slightly. Run a knife around the edge of the tin and turn out the cake. Dust with confectioners' sugar when ready to serve.

½ cup short-grain rice (or pudding rice)

2 cups milk

Pinch of salt

½ stick (4 tablespoons) unsalted butter, plus extra for greasing

Grated rind of ½ lemon

6 tablespoons superfine sugar

3 large eggs, separated

Confectioners' sugar for dusting

Serves 6–8

HERB & OLIVE BREAD

Herb and olive bread makes a satisfying snack when served, either plain or toasted, with slices of cheese and cold meats. For a light meal, add a leafy salad and tangy vinaigrette which can be soaked up by the bread.

6 tablespoons light olive oil, plus extra for greasing

1⅓ cups cornmeal

1 cup brown rice flour

1 teaspoon gluten-free baking powder

1 teaspoon dried fines herbes

1 teaspoon salt

4 large eggs

1 cup buttermilk (or plain yogurt)

1 cup pitted green olives, chopped

Serves 6–8

1   Preheat the oven to 350°F, 180°C, gas mark 4. Grease an 9 x 5-inch non-stick loaf pan with a little oil and line with parchment paper.

2   Mix the cornmeal, rice flour, baking powder, dried herbs and salt in a large bowl.

3   Whisk the eggs in a bowl, then add the buttermilk (or plain yogurt) and olive oil and mix well.

4   Pour the egg mixture on to the flour mixture and stir with a wooden spoon until thoroughly combined. Finally, add the chopped olives.

5   Spoon the loaf mixture into the oiled and lined loaf pan and smooth out the dough. Place in the preheated oven and bake for 50–60 minutes.

6   Use the skewer test (see page 113) to ensure the loaf is cooked through. Allow to cool in the pan slightly, then pass a sharp knife around the edge of the pan and turn out the loaf on to a serving platter. Herb and Olive Bread does not keep well for very long as it tends to dry out, so consume it within two days.

POTATO FLOUR BREAD

This versatile bread is made quickly and easily and is suitable for toasting or for making sandwiches.

3 large eggs, separated

1 cup buttermilk (or plain yogurt)

1½ tablespoons vegetable oil, plus extra for greasing

2 cups potato flour

¾ cup cornmeal

3 teaspoons gluten-free baking powder

1 teaspoon sugar

½ teaspoon salt

Serves 6–8

1   Preheat the oven to 375°F, 190°C, gas mark 5. Grease an 9 x 5-inch non-stick loaf pan with a little oil and line it with parchment paper.

2   Whisk the egg yolks, buttermilk (or yogurt) and oil in a large bowl. Sift in the potato flour, cornmeal, baking powder, sugar and salt and mix well.

3   In a separate bowl, beat the egg whites until stiff but not too dry. Mix a third of this into the batter to loosen it a little, then fold in the rest.

4   Pour the mixture into the prepared loaf pan. Place in the preheated oven and bake for 45 minutes. Use the skewer test (see page 113) to ensure the bread is cooked. Remove the loaf from the oven and allow it to cool in the pan. Then run a knife around the edge of the pan to loosen the loaf and turn out. Serve cut into slices.

CORNBREAD

Made from cornmeal and soured milk, this simple, rustic savory bread (see above) is delicious served alone as a snack, or with stews.

1 Preheat the oven to 400°F, 200°C, gas mark 6. Grease a square 8-inch cake pan with a little oil.

2 Melt the fat in a small saucepan over low heat, then leave to cool. Mix the cornmeal, salt, baking powder and baking soda in a bowl.

3 Add the soured milk or buttermilk, beaten eggs and melted fat. Mix together all of the ingredients until thoroughly combined.

4 Pour into the greased cake pan and bake in the preheated oven for 30 minutes. The bread should be firm to the touch when ready. Serve either warm or cold, cut into squares.

Oil for greasing

½ cup and 2 tablespoons bacon fat, dripping or vegetable shortening

1⅛ cups cornmeal or fine polenta

1 teaspoon salt

1 teaspoon gluten-free baking powder

½ teaspoon baking soda

¾ cup and 1 tablespoon milk with squeeze of lemon juice or buttermilk

2 large eggs, beaten

Serves 6

The analysis for each recipe refers to a single serving, unless stated otherwise. Optional ingredients are not included. The figures are intended as a guide only. If salt is given in a measured amount in the recipe it has been included in the analysis; if the recipe suggests a pinch of salt or seasoning to taste, salt has not been included.

p.12 Tzatziki
80 Cal; 4.5g protein; 6.0g total fat; 13g saturated fat; 2.5g carbohydrate; 0.05g fiber; 47mg sodium; 109mg calcium

p.12 Hummus
284 Cal; 8g protein; 23g total fat; 3g saturated fat; 10g carbohydrate; 3.5g fiber; 16mg sodium; 154mg calcium

p.12 Guacamole
152 Cal; 2g protein; 14g total fat; 3g saturated fat; 4g carbohydrate; 3g fiber; 8mg sodium; 16mg calcium

p.13 Tapenade
224 Cal; 4g protein; 23g total fat; 3g saturated fat; 0g carbohydrate; 2.5g fiber; 2460mg sodium; 91mg calcium

p.14 Melon & Yogurt Soup
72 Cal; 3g protein; 0.5g total fat; 0.2g saturated fat; 15g carbohydrate; 1.5g fiber; 80mg sodium; 91mg calcium

p.14 Gazpacho
281 Cal; 2.5g protein; 24g total fat; 3.5g saturated fat; 11g carbohydrate; 3.5g fiber; 27mg sodium; 31mg calcium

p.14 Ajo Blanco
510 Cal; 10.5g protein; 50g total fat; 5.5g saturated fat; 4g carbohydrate; 4g fiber; 7mg sodium; 120mg calcium

p.16 Carrot & Orange Soup
82 Cal; 1.5g protein; 4g total fat; 0.5g saturated fat; 10g carbohydrate; 2g fiber; 157mg sodium; 38mg calcium

p.16 Eggplant Soup
180 Cal; 4g protein; 12.5g total fat; 2g saturated fat; 14g carbohydrate; 7g fiber; 192mg sodium; 47mg calcium

p.17 Spinach & Lemon Soup
136 Cal; 4.5g protein; 11g total fat; 7g saturated fat; 4g carbohydrate; 3g fiber; 450mg sodium; 224mg calcium

p.17 Rich Tomato Soup
94 Cal; 2.5g protein; 4g total fat; 0.1g saturated fat; 13g carbohydrate; 4g fiber; 52mg sodium; 49mg calcium

p.18 Sweetcorn Soup with Chili Sauce
429 Cal; 4.5g protein; 33.5g total fat; 10g saturated fat; 29g carbohydrate; 2g fiber; 725mg sodium; 18mg calcium

p.19 Avgolemono Soup
114 Cal; 5g protein; 6g total fat; 1.5g saturated fat; 10.5g carbohydrate; 0g fiber; 370mg sodium; 32mg calcium

p.19 Fish Soup with Artichokes
55–44 Cal; 10–8g protein; 0.4–0.3g total fat; 0g saturated fat; 3–2g carbohydrate; 0g fiber; 370–296 mg sodium; 10–8mg calcium

p.20 Squid Salad
596 Cal; 19g protein; 57g total fat; 8g saturated fat; 1g carbohydrate; 0g fiber; 138mg sodium; 16mg calcium

p.20 Seafood Salad
217 Cal; 34g protein; 8.5g total fat; 1.5g saturated fat; 1g carbohydrate; 0.5g fiber; 355mg sodium; 218mg calcium

p.21 Shrimp & Melon Salad
340 Cal; 23g protein; 24g total fat; 3.5g saturated fat; 7g carbohydrate; 1g fiber; 414mg sodium; 123mg calcium

p.23 Mussels with Salsa
60 Cal; 55g protein; 3.5g total fat; 0.5g saturated fat; 2g carbohydrate; 0.7g fiber; 66mg sodium; 65mg calcium

p.23 Sweetcorn Fritters
290 Cal; 7g protein; 18g total fat; 4g saturated fat; 26g carbohydrate; 1g fiber; 248mg sodium; 25mg calcium

p.24 Spinach Roulade
319 Cal; 13g protein; 28g total fat; 16g saturated fat; 3g carbohydrate; 2.5g fiber; 551mg sodium; 282mg calcium

p.25 Molded Gazpacho
50 Cal; 0.5g protein; 4g total fat; 0.5g saturated fat; 3g carbohydrate; 1g fiber; 6mg sodium; 8mg calcium

p.26 Egg & Cucumber Terrine
150 Cal; 9g protein; 11g total fat; 3g saturated fat; 4g carbohydrate; 0.5g fiber; 119mg sodium; 125mg calcium

p.26 Chicken Liver Pâté
165–111 Cal; 11–7.5g protein; 12–8g total fat; 7–5g saturated fat; 2–1g carbohydrate; 0.3–0.2g fiber; 142–95mg sodium; 13–9mg calcium

p.28 Avocado Mousse & Shrimp Sauce
390 Cal; 20g protein; 33g total fat; 6g saturated fat; 3g carbohydrate; 2g fiber; 1201mg sodium; 157mg calcium

p.29 Fish Mousse
140 Cal; 18g protein; 6g total fat; 2g saturated fat; 3g carbohydrate; 0g fiber; 886mg sodium; 92mg calcium

p.32 Baked Cod with Tomatoes
290 Cal; 42g protein; 10.5g total fat; 2g saturated fat; 7g carbohydrate; 2g fiber; 175mg sodium; 54mg calcium

p.33 Fish Pie
563 Cal; 44g protein; 21g total fat; 11g saturated fat; 52g carbohydrate; 2.5g fiber; 823mg sodium; 398mg calcium

p.34 Chicken with Basil & Almonds
543 Cal; 39g protein; 41g total fat; 13g saturated fat; 5g carbohydrate; 2g fiber; 157mg sodium; 176mg calcium

p.34 Chicken, Avocado & Yogurt Mayonnaise
628 Cal; 57g protein; 45g total fat; 10g saturated fat; 6g carbohydrate; 2.5g fiber; 309mg sodium; 127mg calcium

p.35 Chicken Fried with Rosemary & Garlic
382 Cal; 31g protein; 28g total fat; 7g saturated fat; 0g carbohydrate; 0g fiber; 138mg sodium; 13mg calcium

p.36 Endive & Ham Gratin
395 Cal; 25g protein; 31g total fat; 19g saturated fat; 4g carbohydrate; 1g fiber; 797mg sodium; 554mg calcium

p.36 Beef Pie with Olives & Raisins
675–450 Cal; 36–24g protein; 33–22g total fat; 9–6g saturated fat; 61–41g carbohydrate; 5–3g fiber; 784–522mg sodium; 116–77mg calcium

p.37 Beef Salad with Mustard Dressing
590 Cal; 42g protein; 46g total fat; 12g saturated fat; 1g carbohydrate; 0g fiber; 86mg sodium; 24mg calcium

p.37 Pork with Tuna & Yogurt Sauce
272 Cal; 52g protein; 11g total fat; 3g saturated fat; 2g carbohydrate; 232g fiber; 0mg sodium; 59mg calcium

p.39 Soufflé
320 Cal; 18g protein; 24g total fat; 13g saturated fat; 7.5g carbohydrate; 0g fiber; 375mg sodium; 33mg calcium

p.40 Cheese & Onion Tart
868–580 Cal; 27–18g protein; 45–30g total fat; 24–16g saturated fat; 85–66g carbohydrate; 3–2g fiber; 404–270mg sodium; 247–165mg calcium

p.41 Tortilla
295 Cal; 11g protein; 19g total fat; 4g saturated fat; 21g carbohydrate; 2g fiber; 107mg sodium; 52mg calcium

p.43 Risotto
456 Cal; 12g protein; 15g total fat; 9g saturated fat; 62g carbohydrate; 0.5g fiber; 618mg sodium; 182mg calcium

p.44 Risotto Croquettes
224 Cal; 6g protein; 12g total fat; 4g saturated fat; 21g carbohydrate; 0.5g fiber; 227mg sodium; 69mg calcium

p.44 Asparagus Risotto
382 Cal; 8g protein; 8.5g total fat; 1.5g saturated fat; 67g carbohydrate; 1g fiber; 366mg sodium; 62mg calcium

p.46 Polenta
115 Cal; 3g protein; 1g total fat; 0g saturated fat; 23g carbohydrate; 0.7g fiber; 246mg sodium; 1mg calcium

p.47 Polenta Gnocchi
462 Cal; 23g protein; 23g total fat; 12g saturated fat; 41g carbohydrate; 1g fiber; 415mg sodium; 607mg calcium

p.48 Lentil & Grilled Pepper Salad
(For the salad only) 250–200 Cal; 17–13.5g protein; 4.5–3.5g total fat; 1–0.5g saturated fat; 39–31g carbohydrate; 9–7g fiber; 15–12 mg sodium; 69–55mg calcium

(For the dressing: 1 tbsp) 99 Cal; 0g protein; 11g fat; 1.5g saturated fat; 0g carbohydrate, 0g fiber, 0g sodium; 0g calcium

p.49 Lentil & Bacon Stew
532–425 Cal; 26–21g protein; 32–26g total fat; 11–8.5g saturated fat; 37–29g carbohydrate; 7–5.5g fiber; 989–791mg sodium; 72–58mg calcium

p.49 Chickpea Salad with Tuna & Onions
200–160 Cal; 19.5–15.5g protein; 5–4g total fat; 1–0.7g saturated fat; 19–15g carbohydrate; 4–4.5g fiber; 245–196mg sodium; 60–48mg calcium

p.52 Seafood Paella
550 Cal; 28g protein; 10g total fat; 1.5g saturated fat; 59g carbohydrate; 1g fiber; 247mg sodium; 182mg calcium

p.54 Fish Pilaf
520 Cal; 35g protein; 14g total fat; 3g saturated fat; 62g carbohydrate; 0g fiber; 1015mg sodium; 74mg calcium

p.55 Swordfish in Caper & Tomato Sauce
240 Cal; 42g protein; 9g total fat; 2g saturated fat; 7g carbohydrate; 2g fiber; 234mg sodium; 24mg calcium

p.56 Poached Chicken & Vegetables with Red & Green Sauces
(Chicken & vegetables only) 554 Cal; 62g protein; 15g total fat; 5g saturated fat; 44g carbohydrate; 7g fiber; 189mg sodium; 92mg calcium
Salsa Verde 235 Cal; 29g protein; 22g total fat; 2.5g saturated fat; 4g carbohydrate; 4g fiber; 517mg sodium; 194mg calcium
Salsa Rossa 114 Cal; 1.5g protein; 9g total fat; 1g saturated fat; 8g carbohydrate; 2g fiber; 10mg sodium; 18mg calcium

p.58 Chicken Breasts Rolled with Ham & Cheese
400 Cal; 40g protein; 22g total fat; 9g saturated fat; 3g carbohydrate; 0.5g fiber; 417mg sodium; 202mg calcium

p.59 Chicken Breasts Stuffed with Ricotta
410 Cal; 43g protein; 22g total fat; 10g saturated fat; 3g carbohydrate; 0.3g fiber; 303mg sodium; 256mg calcium

p.60 Spiced Beef Stew
350–261 Cal; 39–29g protein; 12–9g total fat; 4–3g saturated fat; 19–14g carbohydrate; 2.4–2g fiber; 122–91mg sodium; 31–23mg calcium

p.60 Braised Steak with Mushrooms
350 Cal; 37g protein; 15g total fat; 5g saturated fat; 3g carbohydrate; 1g fiber; 10mg sodium; 29mg calcium

p.61 Marinated Beef with Olives
470 Cal; 39g protein; 32g total fat; 7g saturated fat; 2g carbohydrate; 1g fiber; 659mg sodium; 26mg calcium

p.62 Stuffed Peppers
340 Cal; 19g protein; 18g total fat; 4g saturated fat; 26g carbohydrate; 3g fiber; 123mg sodium; 116mg calcium

p.63 Meatballs in Tomato & Mushroom Sauce
435–350 Cal; 34–27g protein; 26–21g total fat; 8.5–7g saturated fat; 7–5.5g carbohydrate; 0.7–0.5g fiber; 552–418mg sodium; 40–32mg calcium

p.64 Moroccan Lamb
480 Cal; 44g protein; 21g total fat; 9g saturated fat; 1g carbohydrate; 0g fiber; 486mg sodium; 41mg calcium

p.64 Moussaka
775 Cal; 59g protein; 51g total fat; 20g saturated fat; 22g carbohydrate; 5g fiber; 308mg sodium; 207mg calcium

p.66 Marinated & Grilled Lamb
370 Cal; 35g protein; 25g total fat; 8g saturated fat; 0g carbohydrate; 0g fiber; 123mg sodium; 21mg calcium

p.67 Braised Lamb with Eggplant
390–315 Cal; 38–31g protein; 23–19g total fat; 8–6g saturated fat; 7–5.5g carbohydrate; 3–2g fiber; 494–396mg sodium; 52–41mg calcium

p.68 Pork Tenderloin with Apricots
511 Cal; 41g protein; 16g total fat; 5g saturated fat; 31g carbohydrate; 4g fiber; 453mg sodium; 66mg calcium

p.68 Pork Loin Stuffed with Pâté
527 Cal; 58g protein; 31g total fat; 11.5g saturated fat; 2.4g

carbohydrate; 0g fiber; 1181mg sodium; 28mg calcium

p.72 Potato Gratin
290 Cal; 6g protein; 17g total fat; 11g saturated fat; 30g carbohydrate; 2g fiber; 181mg sodium; 106mg calcium

p.72 Mashed Potatoes with Olive Oil
211 Cal; 4.5g protein; 9g total fat; 2g saturated fat; 30g carbohydrate; 2g fiber; 30mg sodium; 47mg calcium

p.73 Potato Soufflé
400 Cal; 12g protein; 26g total fat; 14g saturated fat; 29g carbohydrate; 2g fiber; 245mg sodium; 65mg calcium

p.73 Spicy Potatoes in Tomato Sauce
215–144 Cal; 4–3g protein; 9–6g total fat; 1–1g saturated fat; 30–20g carbohydrate; 3–2g fiber; 47–32mg sodium; 23–15mg calcium

p.74 Rösti
160 Cal; 3g protein; 5g total fat; 2g saturated fat; 26g carbohydrate; 2g fiber; 29mg sodium; 8mg calcium

p.74 Roast Potatoes with Rosemary & Garlic
211–141 Cal; 3–2g protein; 11–7.5g total fat; 1.5–1g saturated fat; 26–17g carbohydrate; 2–1.3g fiber; 11–7mg sodium; 8–5mg calcium

p.76 Mushrooms with Lemon & Thyme
54 Cal; 1g protein; 5.5g total fat; 1g saturated fat; 0g carbohydrate; 0g fiber; 48mg sodium; 18mg calcium

p.77 Mushrooms Stuffed with Parmesan Cheese
95 Cal; 4g protein; 9g total fat; 2g saturated fat; 3g carbohydrate; 1g fiber; 72mg sodium; 80mg calcium

p.77 Black-eyed Peas with Mushrooms
220–150 Cal; 16–11g protein; 2.5–1.5g total fat; 0.5–0.3g saturated fat; 36–24g carbohydrate; 6–4g fiber; 14–9mg sodium; 61–40mg calcium

p.78 Roasted Vegetables
170–115 Cal; 3.5–2g protein; 12–8g total fat; 2–1g saturated fat; 13–9g carbohydrate; 3.5–5g fiber;

15–10mg sodium; 47–31mg calcium

p.79 Roasted Pepper Salad
90–60 Cal; 2–1g protein; 3.5–2.5g total fat; 0.5–0.5g saturated fat; 13–8.5g carbohydrate; 3–2g fiber; 8–5mg sodium; 16–11mg calcium

p.79 Fried Peppers
125–83 Cal; 1.4–1g protein; 11.5–8g total fat; 2–1g saturated fat; 4.5–3g carbohydrate; 2.8–2g fiber; 7–5mg sodium; 14–9mg calcium

p.80 Fennel with Cheese Sauce
205 Cal; 10g protein; 14g total fat; 9g saturated fat; 11g carbohydrate; 2g fiber; 240mg sodium; 289mg calcium

p.81 Zucchini & Sesame Gratin
172 Cal; 9g protein; 14g total fat; 6g saturated fat; 2g carbohydrate; 1.5g fiber; 170mg sodium; 237mg calcium

p.81 Eggplant Gratin
421 Cal; 22g protein; 33g total fat; 17.5g saturated fat; 8g carbohydrate; 6.5g fiber; 513mg sodium; 574mg calcium

p.82 Green Beans with Garlic & Almonds
155 Cal; 5g protein; 13g total fat; 1.5g saturated fat; 5g carbohydrate; 4g fiber; 2mg sodium; 75mg calcium

p.82 Fennel with Beans
250 Cal; 15g protein; 6.5g total fat, 1g saturated fat; 34g carbohydrate; 6g fiber; 15mg sodium; 61mg calcium

p.83 Fava Beans & Ham
226 Cal; 19g protein; 8g total fat; 1g saturated fat; 19g carbohydrate; 15g fiber; 253mg sodium; 61mg calcium

p.84 Chickpeas with Spinach
245–163 Cal; 11–7g protein; 15–10g total fat; 2–1.5g saturated fat; 18–12g carbohydrate; 7–4.5g fiber; 395–263mg sodium; 257–170mg calcium

p.85 Vegetable "Spaghetti"
76–60 Cal; 1.5–1g protein; 6–4g total fat; 1–0.5g saturated fat; 4–3g carbohydrate; 2–1g fiber; 8–6mg sodium; 27–18mg calcium

p.85 Carrots with Cumin
72–58 Cal; 1.5–1g protein; 3–2.5g total fat; 0.5–0.4g saturated fat; 10–8g carbohydrate; 3–2.5g fiber;

212–169mg sodium; 34–28mg calcium

p.86 Tomato & Artichoke Salad
60–40 Cal; 7.5–5g protein; 0.7–0.5g total fat; 0.3–0.2g saturated fat; 9–6g carbohydrate; 0.8–0.5g fiber; 74–50mg sodium; 108–72mg calcium

p.86 Tomatoes Stuffed with Herb Rice
100 Cal; 3g protein; 5g total fat; 1g saturated fat; 11g carbohydrate; 1g fiber; 30mg sodium; 22mg calcium

p.87 Tomatoes Baked with Parmesan Cheese
120 Cal; 5g protein; 10g total fat; 3.5g saturated fat; 1.5g carbohydrate; 0.5g fiber; 140mg sodium; 154mg calcium

p.88 Lettuce Hearts with Anchovy Dressing
258 Cal; 2.5g protein; 27g total fat; 3.5g saturated fat; 0.5g carbohydrate; 0g fiber; 371mg sodium; 32mg calcium

p.88 Carrots with Raisins & Pine Nuts
291–194 Cal; 3–2g protein; 23–15g total fat; 3–2g saturated fat; 19–13g carbohydrate; 3.5–2g fiber; 90–60mg sodium; 39–26mg calcium

p.90 Mayonnaise
(per 15 ml) 100 Cal; 0.2g protein; 11g total fat; 1.5g saturated fat; 0g carbohydrate; 0g fiber; 76mg sodium; 2mg calcium

p.90 Pesto
(per 15 ml) 120 Cal; 2g protein; 12g total fat; 2g saturated fat; 1g carbohydrate; 0g fiber; 42mg sodium; 73mg calcium

p.91 White Sauce
287 Cal; 10g protein; 12g total fat; 7g saturated fat; 37g carbohydrate; 0g fiber; 178mg sodium; 349mg calcium

p.91 Vinaigrette
(per 15 ml) 83 Cal; 0g protein; 9g total fat; 1g saturated fat; 0g carbohydrate; 0g fiber; 22mg sodium; 0mg calcium

p.94 Rice Pudding Brûlée
243 Cal; 6g protein; 5g total fat; 3g saturated fat; 42g carbohydrate; 0g fiber; 69mg sodium; 149mg calcium

p.94 Fruit Salad Brûlée
190 Cal; 1g protein; 12g total fat; 7.5g saturated fat; 21g carbohydrate; 1g fiber; 12mg sodium; 25mg calcium

p.95 Apricot Soufflé
200–135 Cal; 10–6.5g protein; 8–5g total fat; 2.5–2g saturated fat; 24.5–16g carbohydrate; 3.5–2.5g fiber; 103–69mg sodium; 76–51mg calcium

p.95 Hot Fruit Salad
170 Cal; 1.5g protein; 8g total fat; 5g saturated fat; 25g carbohydrate; 2g fiber; 75mg sodium; 34mg calcium

p.97 Pears Baked in Custard
600–400 Cal; 10–7g protein; 46–31g total fat; 25–17g saturated fat; 39–26g carbohydrate; 5–3.5g fiber; 130–87mg sodium; 107–71mg calcium

p.97 Figs in Honey & Wine
166 Cal; 1.5g protein; 0g total fat; 0g saturated fat; 34g carbohydrate; 1.5g fiber; 8mg sodium; 44mg calcium

p.98 Honey-Poached Oranges
120 Cal; 1.5g protein; 0g total fat; 0g saturated fat; 31g carbohydrate; 2g fiber; 8mg sodium; 57mg calcium

p.98 Orange & Date Salad
130–85 Cal; 3–2g protein; 0g total fat; 0g saturated fat; 30–20g carbohydrate; 5–3g fiber; 15–10mg sodium; 129–86mg calcium

p.98 Orange Crème Caramel
(Using all milk) 230 Cal; 8g protein; 8g total fat; 3g saturated fat; 35g carbohydrate; 0g fiber; 104mg sodium; 120mg calcium

p.101 Vanilla Cheesecake
420–315 Cal; 17–13g protein; 19–14g total fat; 11–8g saturated fat; 47–35g carbohydrate; 0g fiber; 626–469mg sodium; 106–80mg calcium

p.102 Apple Tart
418 Cal; 4g protein; 15g total fat; 9g saturated fat; 68g carbohydrate; 2.5g fiber; 147mg sodium; 18mg calcium

p.103 Lemon Custard Tart
470 Cal; 10g protein; 29g total fat; 16g saturated fat; 44g carbohydrate; 0.6g fiber; 146mg sodium; 48mg calcium

p.104 Almond Meringue Gâteau
500 Cal; 8g protein; 34g total fat; 13g saturated fat; 43g carbohydrate; 2g fiber; 60mg sodium; 83mg calcium

p.105 Rolled Coconut Meringue
475–356 Cal; 4–3g protein; 25–19g total fat; 18.5–14g saturated fat; 61–46g carbohydrate; 2.5–2g fiber; 94–71mg sodium; 24–18mg calcium

p.106 Vanilla Ice Cream
225 Cal; 4.5g protein; 19g total fat; 11g saturated fat; 9g carbohydrate; 0g fiber; 58mg sodium; 39mg calcium

p.106 Chocolate Chip Ice Cream with Raspberry Sauce
375 Cal; 3.5g protein; 25g total fat; 15g saturated fat; 35g carbohydrate; 1g fiber; 49mg sodium; 39mg calcium

p.107 Strawberry Sorbet
90–59 Cal; 2.5–1.5g protein; 0g total fat; 0g saturated fat; 21–14g carbohydrate; 1.5–1g fiber; 38–25mg sodium; 21–14mg calcium

p.107 Coffee Praline Mousse
240 Cal; 10g protein; 14.5g total fat; 8g saturated fat; 18g carbohydrate; 0g fiber; 105mg sodium; 136mg calcium

p.108 Lemon Curd
(per 15 ml) 60 Cal; 1g protein; 3g total fat; 1.5g saturated fat; 8g carbohydrate; 0g fiber; 27mg sodium; 4mg calcium

p.108 English Custard Sauce
(per 600 ml) 663 Cal; 32g protein; 34g total fat; 16.5g saturated fat; 61g carbohydrate; 0g fiber; 468mg sodium; 681mg calcium

p.112 Chocolate Hazelnut Cake
1048–786 Cal; 18–13.5g protein; 81–61g total fat; 34–25g saturated fat; 67–50g carbohydrate; 3–2g fiber; 374–281mg sodium; 176–132mg calcium

p.113 Chocolate Roulade
320 Cal; 5g protein; 21g total fat; 12g saturated fat; 28g carbohydrate; 0g fiber; 60mg sodium; 37mg calcium

p.114 Chocolate Walnut Cake
660–500 Cal; 20–15g protein; 44–33g total fat; 10–7g saturated fat; 50–37g carbohydrate; 1.5–1g fiber; 476–375mg sodium; 123–93mg calcium

p.114 Lemon Polenta & Almond Cake
772–580 Cal; 15–11g protein; 54–40g total fat; 22–17g saturated fat; 59–44g carbohydrate; 3–2.5g fiber; 435–326mg sodium; 120–90mg calcium

p.115 Almond Sponge Cake
410–305 Cal; 12.5–9g protein; 22.5–17g total fat; 3.5–2.5g saturated fat; 41–31g carbohydrate; 2–1.5g fiber; 82–61mg sodium; 100–75mg calcium

p.117 Orange & Almond Cake
515–390 Cal; 16–12g protein; 28–21g total fat; 4–3g saturated fat; 52–40g carbohydrate; 4–3g fiber; 100–75mg sodium; 159–119mg calcium

p.118 Date & Brown Sugar Muffins
(per large muffin) 270 Cal; 6.5g protein; 10g total fat; 5g saturated fat; 39g carbohydrate; 1g fiber; 212mg sodium; 73mg calcium

p.120 Fruit & Nut Loaf
610–460 Cal; 8–6g protein; 33–27g total fat; 20–15g saturated fat; 66–49g carbohydrate; 1.5–1g fiber; 393–295mg sodium; 36–27mg calcium

p.121 Sand Cake
580–435 Cal; 6–4.5g protein; 36–27g total fat; 20–15g saturated fat; 62–46g carbohydrate; 1–0.5g fiber; 317–238mg sodium; 48–36mg calcium

p.121 Rice Cake
275–210 Cal; 8–6g protein; 14–11g total fat; 8–6g saturated fat; 30–23g carbohydrate; 0g fiber; 157–118mg sodium; 118–89mg calcium

p.122 Herb & Olive Bread
350–260 Cal; 11–8g protein; 15.5–11.5g total fat; 3–2g saturated fat; 40–30g carbohydrate; 1.5–1g fiber; 862–647mg sodium; 96–72mg calcium

p.122 Potato Flour Bread
290–220 Cal; 11–8g protein; 7–5.5g total fat; 1.5–1g saturated fat; 47–35g carbohydrate; 3–2g fiber; 479–359mg sodium; 100–75mg calcium

p.123 Cornbread
340 Cal; 6.5g protein; 24g total fat; 12g saturated fat; 23g carbohydrate; 0.5g fiber; 568mg sodium; 60mg calcium

Index

ACKNOWLEDGMENTS

Carroll & Brown would
particularly like to thank: Leon
H. Rottmann and the Celiac
Sprue Association of the USA
for their expert advice and
invaluable comments on the
manuscript; and Victoria
Spencer for so carefully
Americanizing the recipes.

Food preparation: Michael Cox
Art director: Denise Brown
Nutritional analysis: Fiona
Hunter

Thanks also to Laura Price,
Dawn Henderson and Charlotte
Beech for their assistance.